200 pies a

hamlyn | **all colour cookbook**

200
Sara Lewis

pies and tarts

An Hachette UK Company
www.hachette.co.uk

First published in Great Britain in 2012 by Hamlyn
a division of Octopus Publishing Group Ltd
Endeavour House, 189 Shaftesbury Avenue
London WC2H 8JY
www.octopusbooks.co.uk

ISBN 978-0-60062-354-0

A CIP catalogue record for this book is available from the
British Library

Printed and bound in China

10 9 8 7 6 5 4 3 2 1

Both metric and imperial measurements have been given in all
recipes. Use one set of measurements only, and not a mixture
of both.

Standard level spoon measurements are used in all recipes
1 tablespoon = 15 ml spoon
1 teaspoon = 5 ml spoon

Ovens should be preheated to the specified temperature –
if using a fan-assisted oven, follow the manufacturer's
instructions for adjusting the time and temperature.

Fresh herbs should be used unless otherwise stated.
Medium eggs should be used unless otherwise stated.

Some recipes are specified for those following a gluten-free
diet. It is prudent to check the labels of all pre-prepared
ingredients for the inclusion of any ingredients that may
contain gluten as different brands may vary.

This book includes dishes made with nuts and nut derivatives.
It is advisable for those with known allergic reactions to nuts
and nut derivatives or those who may be potentially vulnerable
to these allergies, such as pregnant and nursing mothers,
invalids, the elderly, babies and children to avoid dishes made
with these. It is prudent to check the labels of all pre-prepared
ingredients for the possible inclusion of nut derivatives.

contents

introduction

introduction

Home baking is making a resurgence. We all seem to lead such busy lives now that rediscovering the joys of cooking is not only relaxing and rewarding, but home cooking can also taste so much better than the shop-bought version. Over the next few pages you will find a range of recipes from tiny bite-sized pies and tarts made in a mini muffin tin to picnic pies that can be added to school or work lunchboxes, savoury tarts for a midweek supper or a special Saturday supper, to melt-in-the-mouth fruit pies and tarts that will remind you of holidays abroad or perhaps nostalgic memories of mum's or granny's cooking. There is also a chapter for gluten-free pies and tarts, so that those on a special diet need not miss out. Making pastry is not as tricky as some new cooks may think; the secret is to have a good set of scales and measuring spoons so that you can measure out ingredients accurately. You also need to chill the pastry after making and to roll out on a surface lightly dusted with flour so that the pastry doesn't stick. If you don't have time to make your own pastry, however, don't worry, you can still make the recipes – just cheat a little and use a pack of ready-made from the supermarket.

Shortcrust pastry

A great versatile everyday pastry. The secret is to keep everything cool, to use a light touch and to handle as little as possible. Add just enough water to mix, allowing 1 teaspoon per 25 g (1 oz) of flour – too much and the pastry will be sticky and taste hard when baked.

Makes 470 g (15 oz)
Enough to make:
- A deep 20 cm (8 inch) pie with a lattice decoration
- Or six 10 cm (4 inch) tarts
- Or 12 muffin-sized tarts
- Or line four 13 cm (5 inch) tart tins
- Or line a 24 cm (9½ inch) × 2.5 cm (1 inch) deep tart tin

250 g (8 oz) **plain flour**
125 g (4 oz) half **butter** and half white **vegetable fat** or **lard**, or all **butter**, diced
2½–3 tablespoons **cold water**
salt

Add the flour and a pinch of salt to a large mixing bowl. Add the fats and rub them into the flour with your fingertips or use a freestanding electric mixer until the mixture resembles fine crumbs.

Gradually mix in just enough water to enable the crumbs to be squeezed together to form a soft but not sticky dough.

Knead very lightly until smooth, then roll out on a lightly floured surface and use to line a tart case or to top a pie.

For flavour variations, try adding 1 teaspoon dry English mustard, a few chopped fresh herbs or 40 g (1½ oz) freshly grated Parmesan or mature Cheddar cheese.

For sweet shortcrust pastry, add 50 g (2 oz) caster sugar to the bowl with the flour and salt and use 125 g (4 oz) butter instead of a mix of butter and white vegetable fat or lard. Continue as above.

For 12 double crust mini muffin sized pies or 6 double crust 10 cm (4 inch) pies, make up the pastry using 375 g (12 oz) plain flour, a pinch of salt, 175 g (6 oz) half butter and half white vegetable fat or lard, or all butter and about 4 tablespoons cold water. For sweet pies, add 75 g (3 oz) caster sugar and all butter and not a mixture of fats.

To make 24 mini muffin sized tart cases, reduce the pastry to 175 g (6 oz) plain flour, 75 g (3 oz) butter or a mix of butter and white vegetable fat or lard and 2 tablespoons cold water.

Pâte sucrée

This French-style pastry is richer than shortcrust as it contains butter and egg yolks to bind instead of water. It is traditionally made straight on to the work surface by mounding up the flour, then making a dip in the centre. Add the sugar, soft butter and egg yolks to the centre, then work with your fingertips, drawing in more of the flour until it is all incorporated into a soft dough. Using a food processor, electric mixer or bowl is much easier and less messy.

Makes 375 g (12 oz)

Enough to make:
- A 24 cm (9½ inch) tart
- Or a 20 cm (8 inch) tart that is 5 cm (2 inches) deep
- Or 12 muffin-sized tarts
- Or 24 mini muffin-sized tart cases

175 g (6 oz) **plain flour**
40 g (1½ oz) **icing sugar**
100 g (3½ oz) **butter**, diced
2 **egg yolks**

Add the flour, icing sugar and butter to a food processor or mixing bowl and mix until you have fine crumbs. Add the egg yolks and mix together until you have a soft ball. Wrap in clingfilm and chill for 15 minutes before using.
For flavour variations, try adding the grated rind of 1 small orange or 1 lemon, or 1 teaspoon ground cinnamon; or substitute 15 g (½ oz) of the flour for 15 g (½ oz) of sifted cocoa powder; or add 40 g (½ oz) finely chopped hazelnuts when adding the egg yolks.

Hot water crust pastry

This traditional British pastry is made in a completely different way by warming lard in milk, then mixing it into flour. When it has cooled, it can be pressed into a tin or moulded over a greased jar or pie mould and chilled until set, then filled, topped with a pastry lid and baked. It is a much more robust pastry that doesn't require such a light touch.

Makes 750 g (1½ lb)

Enough to make:
- Six individual pies
- Or one large round 18 cm (7 inch) pie

175 g (6 oz) **lard**
175 ml (6 fl oz) **milk**, or half milk and half water
375 g (12 oz) **plain flour**
¼ teaspoon **salt**

Add the lard and milk (or milk and water mix) to a saucepan and heat gently until the lard has just melted. Bring just to the boil, then tip into a bowl containing the flour and salt and mix with a wooden spoon until it forms a smooth soft ball.
Cover the top of the bowl with a clean cloth and leave until cool enough to handle (about 10–20 minutes).
Knead lightly, then shape and bake according to the chosen recipe.
For flavour variations, try adding ¼ teaspoon cayenne pepper or 1 teaspoon English mustard powder when adding the flour and salt; or for a sweet version add 50 g (2 oz) caster sugar when melting the lard in the milk.

Gluten-free pastry

If you have an intolerance to gluten, rice flour or wheat-free bread flour can be used instead of wheat flour. Unlike with wheat flour, the pastry is quite crumbly, so does require careful handling; it can either be rolled out between two sheets of clingfilm or pressed directly into a greased tin. If the pastry does crack, simply press it back together again or patch with extra pieces of pastry, sticking in place with beaten egg, milk or water.

Makes 325 g (11 oz)
Enough to make:

- Six 10 cm (4 inch) tart tins
- Or line a 24 cm (9½ inch) tart tin
- Or to cover four 300 ml (½ pint) individual pie dishes
- Or a 1.2 litre (2 pint) pie dish

175 g (6 oz) **rice flour**
pinch of **salt**
100 g (3½ oz) **butter**, diced
2 **egg yolks**
2 teaspoons **cold water**

Add the rice flour, salt and butter to a mixing bowl and rub in with your fingertips or an electric mixer until you have fine crumbs. Add the egg yolks and mix to a soft dough, adding the water as required.
Roll out between two pieces of clingfilm or press into a greased tart tin as required (see page 14).
For sweet gluten-free pastry, add 40 g (1½ oz) icing sugar to the flour.

Cheat with bought pastry

Puff pastry and filo pastry are so good that it is really not worth making your own. Keep a handy supply in the freezer, and remember to take it out in plenty of time so that the pastry can defrost at room temperature. When using puff pastry, try to keep an even pressure when rolling out so that the finished pie will rise evenly. Sprinkle the work surface only very lightly with flour - just enough that it won't stick but not so much that the pastry becomes dry. Filo pastry can dry out very quickly as the sheets are wafer thin. If shaping tiny boureks, unfold the pastry, but keep the remaining stack covered with clingfilm or a teacloth and try to use as quickly as possible.

If you are very short of time, you may prefer to use ready-made shortcrust pastry, which is available chilled or frozen, plain or sweet, and makes a perfectly acceptable alternative to homemade pastry.

Tips & techniques

Lining a pastry case

A loose-bottomed tart tin makes it easy to remove the finished tart after baking.

Roll out the pastry on a lightly floured surface a little larger than the tin. Lift over a rolling pin and drape into the tin.

Press over the base and up the sides of the tin with your fingertips, taking care where the sides meet the base.

Trim off the excess pastry with a knife a little above the top of the tin, to allow for shrinkage either before or after baking.

14

Baking blind

This rather strange term really just means
to bake the tart case empty.

Prick the base of the pastry
case with a fork. Chill for
15 minutes to allow the
pastry to 'relax'; this will
help to minimize shrinkage
during baking.

Line the tart case with
a piece of crumpled
greaseproof or nonstick
baking paper that is large
enough to cover the base
and sides of the tart.
Add a generous layer of
baking beans – available
from the cookware
department of large
department stores, specialist
cookware shops and some
larger supermarkets – or
improvise and use some
dried pasta or pulses.

Put the tart on a baking sheet and bake in a preheated oven,
190°C (375°F), Gas Mark 5, for 10–15 minutes for a large
tart, 8–10 minutes for individual tarts and 5 minutes for mini
muffin sized tarts, until the case is just set, then carefully lift
the paper and beans out of the tart case and cook empty for
5 minutes for a large tart, 4–5 minutes for individual tarts and
2–3 minutes for mini muffin sized tarts until the base is dry
and crisp and the top edges of the tart are pale golden.

Covering and decorating a pie

For a professional finish to a puff or shortcrust topped meat or fruit pie.

Cut a narrow strip of pastry from the edges of the rolled-out dough, the same width as the rim of the pie dish. Brush the rim with water, beaten egg or milk and stick the pastry strips in place, butting the ends of the strips together until the rim is completely covered.

Brush the strips with water, egg or milk once more, then lift the remaining pastry over a rolling pin and drape over the top of the pie. Press the edges together to create a seal, then trim off the excess pastry with a small knife.

Knock up the edges of the pie by making small horizontal cuts around the edge of the pastry rim. This helps to encourage the puff pastry layers to separate and rise during baking and can also give the impression of layers in a shortcrust pie.

Flute the edges by pressing the first and second finger on to the pie edge, then make small cuts with a knife between them to create a scalloped edge. Repeat all the way around the pie. Brush the pie with a little beaten or milk to glaze it.

To decorate with pastry leaves, reroll the pastry trimmings if needed and cut a strip about 2.5 cm (1 inch) wide, then cut out diamond shapes. Mark veins with the knife, then curl the ends of the leaf and position on the glazed pie. Alternatively, hearts, circles, festive shapes or numbers can be stamped from rerolled pastry trimmings with small biscuit cutters, then arranged on the glazed pie. Glaze the decorations with a little more beaten egg or milk before baking. For smaller pies, it can also be effective to stamp out small holes with cutters so that the filling can be seen.

bite-sized snacks

pissaldiere bites

Makes **18**
Preparation time **25 minutes**
Cooking time **25–30 minutes**

2 tablespoons **olive oil**, plus
  extra to serve (optional)
250 g (8 oz) **onions**, thinly
  sliced
1 **garlic clove**, finely chopped
1 teaspoon **caster sugar**
small bunch of **thyme**
250 g (8 oz) **ready-made puff
  pastry**, defrosted if frozen
1 **beaten egg**, to glaze
9 **anchovy fillets** from a can,
  drained
9 small **stuffed green olives**
salt and **pepper**

Heat the oil in a frying pan, add the onions and fry
gently for 10 minutes until soft and just beginning to
colour. Add the garlic and sugar and fry for a further
5 minutes until golden. Take the pan off the heat, tear
leaves from half the thyme over the onion and season
with salt and pepper.

Roll the pastry out on a lightly floured surface and trim
to a 15 × 30 cm (6 × 12 inch) rectangle, then cut into
5 cm (2 inch) squares. Transfer the squares to an oiled
baking sheet, leaving a little space between them.

Brush the tops with beaten egg, then divide the onion
mix between them. Cut each anchovy fillet into 2 thin
strips and arrange 2 on each pastry square as a cross,
then top with a halved olive.

Bake in a preheated oven, 200°C (400°F), Gas Mark 6,
for 10–15 minutes until the pastry is well risen and
golden. Brush the olives with a little extra oil, if liked,
and sprinkle with the remaining thyme leaves. Serve
warm or cold with drinks.

For feta & red pepper bites, top the pastry squares
with a mix of 1 onion, thinly sliced and fried in
1 tablespoon olive oil until golden, 1 garlic clove,
finely chopped, 125 g (4 oz) roasted red peppers
from a jar, drained and thinly sliced, 100 g (4 oz) feta
cheese, crumbled, a few thyme leaves, and salt and
pepper. Bake as above.

spinach boureks

Makes **36**
Preparation time **30 minutes**
Cooking time **15 minutes**

400 g (13 oz) **frozen spinach**,
   just defrosted
250 g (8 oz) **cream cheese**
2 **garlic cloves**, finely
   chopped
1 **egg**, beaten
a little **grated nutmeg**
6 sheets **filo pastry**,
   48 × 23 cm (19 × 9 inches),
   from a 270 g (8¾ oz) pack,
   defrosted
100 g (3½ oz) **butter**, melted
salt and **pepper**

Add the spinach to a sieve set over a bowl and press out the juices with the back of a spoon. In another bowl, mix the cream cheese, garlic and egg together. Stir in the spinach and season with nutmeg, salt and pepper.

Unfold the pastry sheets and put one sheet on the work surface with the long edge facing you. Cover the remaining sheets with clingfilm so that they don't dry out. Brush the pastry in front of you with a little melted butter, then cut into 6 strips, 7.5 × 23 cm (3 × 9 inches). Put a teaspoon of the spinach mixture near the bottom right corner of each strip.

Holding the bottom right corner of one of the strips, lift and fold up and over diagonally to make a triangular shape to enclose the filling. Fold the bottom left corner straight upwards to make a thicker triangle, then continue folding until you reach the top of the pastry.

Make 5 more boureks, then take a second sheet of pastry and repeat. Continue until all the pastry and filling has been used up. Transfer to a baking sheet and brush with the remaining butter. Bake in a preheated oven, 180°C (350°F), Gas Mark 4, for 15 minutes until golden. Leave to cool slightly, then serve warm or cold.

For aubergine boureks, fry 1 chopped onion and 1 diced aubergine in 2 tablespoons olive oil until softened. Add 2 finely chopped garlic cloves and a 400 g (13 oz) can chopped tomatoes, 1 teaspoon caster sugar, ¼ teaspoon ground allspice and salt and pepper. Cover and simmer for 15–20 minutes until the aubergine is soft. Leave to cool, then make up the boureks with pastry and butter and cook as above.

mini harissa sausage rolls

Makes **30**
Preparation time **30 minutes**
Cooking time **20 minutes**

500 g (1 lb) good-quality **pork
    sausagemeat**
50 g (2 oz) **walnut pieces**,
    roughly chopped
5 cm (2 inch) **fresh root
    ginger**, peeled and coarsely
    grated
1 teaspoon **black
    peppercorns**, roughly
    crushed
500 g (1 lb) **ready-made puff
    pastry**, defrosted if frozen
beaten egg, to glaze
3 teaspoons **harissa paste**
salt

Add the sausagemeat, walnuts and ginger to a large
bowl, sprinkle over the pepper and a little salt, then
mix together with a wooden spoon or your hands.

Roll the pastry out thinly on a lightly floured surface
and trim to a 30 cm (12 inch) square. Cut the square
into 3 strips, 10 cm (4 inches) wide, then brush lightly
with beaten egg. Spread 1 teaspoon of harissa in a
band down the centre of each pastry strip, then top
each strip with one-third of the sausagemeat mixture,
spooning into a narrow band.

Fold the pastry over the filling and press the edges
together well with the flattened tip of a small sharp
knife. Trim the edge to neaten if needed, then slash
the top of the strips.

Brush the sausage rolls with beaten egg, then cut each
strip into 10 pieces and arrange slightly spaced apart
on 2 lightly oiled baking sheets. Cook in a preheated
oven, 200°C (400°F), Gas Mark 6, for about 20 minutes
until golden and the pastry is well risen. Transfer to a
wire rack then leave to cool for 20 minutes. Serve warm
or cold.

For curried sausage rolls, omit the walnuts from
the sausagemeat filling, adding 50 g (2 oz) sultanas,
1 teaspoon turmeric, 2 chopped garlic cloves and
2 tablespoons chopped coriander. Spread each pastry
strip with 1 teaspoon mild curry paste, then top with
the sausagemeat mixture, shape and bake as above.

mini filo & guacamole cups

Makes **16**
Preparation time **30 minutes**
Cooking time **4–5 minutes**

1 sheet of **filo pastry**,
   48 × 23 cm (19 × 9 inches),
   from a 270 g (8¾ oz) pack,
   defrosted if frozen
25 g (1 oz) **butter**, melted
1 ripe **avocado**
juice of **1 lime**
½ mild **red chilli**, deseeded
   and finely chopped, plus
   extra to garnish
1 **spring onion**, finely
   chopped
2 tablespoons finely chopped
   coriander, plus extra to
   garnish
salt and **pepper**

Unfold the pastry sheet, brush with butter, then cut into 32 small squares about 5 cm (2 inches) each. Gently press 1 square into 16 sections of 2 × 12-section mini muffin tins, then add a second square of pastry to each at right angles to the first for a petal-like effect.

Bake in a preheated oven, 190°C (375°F), Gas Mark 5, for 4–5 minutes until golden. Lift the filo cups out of the tins and cool on a wire rack.

Halve, stone and peel the avocado, then mash with the lime juice or blitz in a food processor. Add the chilli, spring onion and coriander, season lightly with salt and pepper and mix together.

Spoon the guacamole into the filo cups, garnish with extra chopped chilli and coriander, if liked, and serve within 1 hour of finishing as the avocado discolours.

For mini filo & taramasalata cups, make the cups as above, then fill with 200 g (7 oz) chilled taramasalata and garnish with a few chopped black olives and a little chopped parsley.

parmesan & tomato tarts

Makes **24**
Preparation time **30 minutes**,
  plus chilling
Cooking time **18–20 minutes**

2 **eggs**
150 ml (¼ pint) **milk**
50 g (2 oz) **Parmesan
  cheese**, finely grated
3 **spring onions**, finely
  chopped
8 small **cherry tomatoes**,
  thickly sliced
salt and **pepper**
tiny **basil leaves**, to garnish

For the pastry
175 g (6 oz) **plain flour**
75 g (3 oz) **butter**, diced
2 tablespoons chopped **basil**
2 tablespoons **cold water**

Make the pastry. Add the flour, a little salt and pepper and the butter to a mixing bowl, then rub in the butter with your fingertips or using an electric mixer until you have fine crumbs. Add the basil, then mix in enough water to form a soft but not sticky dough.

Knead the pastry lightly, then roll it out thinly on a lightly floured surface. Stamp out 24 x 6 cm (2½ inch) circles with a plain biscuit cutter, then press into the buttered sections of 2 × 12-section mini muffin tins, rerolling the trimmings as needed. Chill for 15 minutes.

Fork the eggs and milk together in a bowl. Add the Parmesan, spring onions and a little salt and pepper and mix well. Spoon into the tarts, then add a slice of tomato to each one.

Bake in a preheated oven, 180°C (350°F), Gas Mark 4, for 18–20 minutes until golden and the filling is just set. Leave to stand for 10 minutes, then loosen the edges of the tarts and remove from the tins. Garnish with tiny basil leaves just before serving.

For Parmesan & prawn tarts, omit the sliced tomatoes from the tarts and add 1 small cooked peeled prawn, defrosted if frozen, to each instead. Bake as above.

medieval spiced steak pies

Makes **24**
Preparation time **30 minutes**,
  plus chilling
Cooking time **15 minutes**

1 quantity **plain shortcrust
  pastry** (see page 9)
beaten egg, to glaze
sifted **icing sugar**, for dusting

For the filling
100 ml (3½ fl oz) **brandy**
100 g (3½ oz) **currants**
100 g (3½ oz) **raisins**
40 g (1½ oz) **glacé or stem
  ginger**, chopped
grated rind of ½ **orange**
grated rind of ½ **lemon**
½ teaspoon **ground mixed
  spice**
¼ teaspoon **grated nutmeg**
50 g (2 oz) **blanched
  almonds**, chopped
200 g (7 oz) **extra lean
  minced beef**
100 g (3½ oz) **shredded suet**
1 **tart dessert apple**, cored
  and grated

Make the filling. Pour the brandy into a saucepan, bring just to the boil, then add the dried fruits, ginger, fruit rinds and spices and leave to cool. Mix in the almonds, beef, suet and apple, then cover and leave in the refrigerator overnight so that the flavours can develop.

Next day, roll out two-thirds of the pastry on a lightly floured surface and stamp out 7.5 cm (3 inch) circles with a plain biscuit cutter. Press into the buttered sections of 2 × 12-section bun tins, rerolling the pastry as needed. Spoon in the filling.

Add any pastry trimmings to the reserved pastry, then roll out and stamp out 24 × 6 cm (2½ inch) plain circles for the pie tops, rerolling the trimmings as needed. Brush the edges of the filled pie bases with beaten egg, add the lids and press the edges together well.

Brush the tops with beaten egg, then make 4 small steam vents. Bake in a preheated oven, 190°C (375°F), Gas Mark 5, for 15 minutes until the pastry is golden. Leave to stand for 10 minutes, then loosen the edges of the pastry and transfer to a wire rack to cool. Just before serving, dust the tops lightly with sifted icing sugar. These are delicious served as a savoury starter before the Christmas roast turkey or a special roast dinner.

For traditional dessert mince pies, omit the 200 g (7 oz) minced beef and add 125 g (4 oz) sultanas and 75 g (3 oz) light muscovado sugar. Continue as above.

feta & spring onion cigarellos

Makes **18**
Preparation time **25 minutes**
Cooking time **10–12 minutes**

200 g (7 oz) **feta cheese**,
   drained and coarsely grated
3 **spring onions**, very finely
   chopped
3 tablespoons **Greek yogurt**
1 **egg**, beaten
3 sheets of **filo pastry**,
   48 × 23 cm (19 × 9 inches),
   from a 270 g (8¾ oz) pack,
   defrosted if frozen
50 g (2 oz) **butter**, melted
3 tablespoons **sesame
   seeds**, for sprinkling
   (optional)
pepper

Beat the feta, onions, yogurt and egg together and season with a little pepper. Spoon into a piping bag fitted with a large plain nozzle.

Unfold the pastry sheets and put one sheet on your work surface with the long edge facing you. Brush with a little of the butter, then cut into 3 strips, 15 × 23 cm (6 × 9 inches), then cut in half to make 15 × 11 cm (6 × 4½ inch) rectangles.

Pipe a line of the feta cheese mixture about 2.5 cm (1 inch) up from the long side of each rectangle and a little in from the short sides. Fold the short sides in, then the base of the pastry, and roll up to enclose the filling completely and make a thin cigar-type shape. Continue until you have 6 cigarellos from the sheet of pastry.

Repeat with the remaining pastry sheets and feta mixture until both are used up. Arrange on an ungreased baking sheet and brush the outside of each with the remaining butter. Sprinkle with a few sesame seeds, if liked. Bake in a preheated oven, 190°C (375°F), Gas Mark 5, for 10–12 minutes until the pastry is golden brown.

Leave to cool, then serve while still warm with salad as a starter or glasses of chilled wine as an aperitif.

For pesto cigarellos, brush each pastry sheet with a little melted butter, then spread very thinly with red pesto (you will need 3 tablespoons in total). Pipe on the feta mixture and continue as above. Shape and brush with remaining butter and sprinkle with a few salt flakes instead of the sesame seeds before baking.

samosas

Makes **18**
Preparation time **30 minutes**
Cooking time **35–45 minutes**

2 medium **baking potatoes**,
  about 300 g (10 oz) in total,
  scrubbed
2 tablespoons **sunflower oil**,
1 **onion**, finely chopped
1½ teaspoons **black mustard
  seeds**
2 teaspoons **cumin seeds**,
  roughly crushed
2 **Thai green chillies**, with
  seeds, finely chopped
1 teaspoon **coriander seeds**,
  crushed
3 tablespoons chopped
  coriander
¼ teaspoon **turmeric**
75 g (3 oz) **frozen peas**,
  defrosted
1 litre **sunflower oil**, for deep
  frying
salt and **pepper**

For the pastry
200 g (7 oz) **plain flour**
50 g (2 oz) **butter or ghee**,
  diced
4–5 tablespoons **cold water**

Cook the potatoes whole in boiling water for 15–20 minutes until tender. Drain and leave until cool enough to handle, then peel off the skins and dice the flesh.

Heat the oil in the drained and dried potato pan, add the onion and fry for 3 minutes, then add the mustard seeds, cumin seeds and green chillies and cook for 2 minutes. Mix in the crushed and chopped coriander, turmeric, then the potatoes, peas and plenty of salt and pepper.

Make the pastry. Add the flour, a little salt and the butter or ghee to a mixing bowl, rub in the butter with your fingertips until you have fine crumbs, then mix in enough of the water to form a soft but not sticky dough. Knead well until smooth and elastic. Cut into 9 pieces and shape into balls. Roll out to 12 cm (5 inch) circles.

Cut each circle in half, brush the edges with water, then shape into a cone by folding one point to the centre of the curved top; do the same with the other point. Spoon the filling into the cone, then press the curved edges together to seal. Repeat to make 18 samosas.

Half fill a large saucepan with oil, heat to 180°C (350°F) on a sugar thermometer or until the oil bubbles when a samosa is dropped into the oil. Cook the samosas in batches of 3 or 4 for 3–4 minutes until golden brown, then lift out and transfer to a plate lined with kitchen paper. Serve warm with mango chutney or cucumber raita.

For gingered prawn samosas, reduce the amount of potato to 300 g (7 oz), cook as above, then add 2.5 cm (1 inch) fresh root ginger, peeled and grated along with the chillies. Mix in 100 g (3½ oz) small cooked peeled prawns, defrosted if frozen, with the peas.

papaya, lime & mango tartlets

Makes **20**
Preparation time **35 minutes**,
    plus chilling
Cooking time **15–20 minutes**

250 g (8 oz) chilled ready-
    made or homemade **sweet**
    shortcrust pastry (see
    page 10) **or pâte sucrée**
    (see page 11)
thinly grated rind and juice of
    2 large, juicy **limes**
6 tablespoons **double cream**
150 ml (¼ pint) **full-fat**
    condensed milk
2 tablespoons finely diced
    mango
2 tablespoons finely diced
    papaya
lime rind, to decorate

Roll the pastry out on a lightly floured surface to 2.5 mm (⅛ inch) thickness, then, stamp out 20 x 5 cm (2 inch) circles using a plain biscuit cutter. Use the circles to line 20 x 5 cm (2 inch) mini tartlet tins. Prick the pastry bases with a fork. Chill. Line the tartlets with squares of nonstick baking paper and baking beans and bake blind in a preheated oven, 190°C (375°F), Gas Mark 5, for 10 minutes, then remove the paper and beans and return the cases to the oven for 8–10 minutes or until they are crisp and golden. Remove the cases from the tin and cool on a wire rack.

Put the lime rind in a blender with the cream and condensed milk and pulse until well combined. With the motor running, slowly pour in the lime juice and process until blended. (Alternatively, mix well by hand.) Transfer to a bowl, cover and chill for 3–4 hours or until firm.

Put the cases on a serving platter and spoon the lime mixture into each case. Mix the mango with the papaya and, using a teaspoon, fill the cases. Decorate with lime rind and serve immediately.

For summer berry tartlets, make the pastry cases and filling as above. Spoon the lime mixture into the cases. Warm 3 tablespoons redcurrant jelly with the grated rind and juice of 1 lime, cook until syrupy, then stir in 150 g (5 oz) blueberries and 150 g (5 oz) raspberries. Spoon over the top of the tartlets.

mini chocolate truffle tarts

Makes **24**

Preparation time **30 minutes**, plus chilling

Cooking time **9–10 minutes**

1 quantity **pâte sucrée** (see page 11), chilled
250 ml (8 fl oz) **double cream**
2 tablespoons **icing sugar**
200 g (7 oz) **plain dark chocolate**, broken into pieces
4 tablespoons **brandy**
chocolate curls, to decorate
sifted **icing sugar**, for dusting (optional)

Roll the pastry out thinly on a lightly floured surface, then stamp out 24 × 6 cm (2½ inch) circles with a fluted biscuit cutter and press into the buttered sections of 2 × 12-section mini muffin tin. Reknead and reroll the pastry trimmings as needed. Prick the base of each tart 2–3 times with a fork, then chill for 15 minutes.

Line the tarts with small squares of nonstick baking paper and baking beans and bake in a preheated oven, 190°C (375°F), Gas Mark 5, for 5 minutes. Remove the paper and beans and cook for a further 4–5 minutes until the bases are crisp. Remove the cases from the tins and cool on a wire rack.

Pour the cream into a small saucepan, add the sugar and bring just to the boil. Take off the heat, add the chocolate and leave for 5 minutes until melted. Stir until smooth, then gradually mix in the brandy. Leave to cool, then transfer to the refrigerator for about 1 hour until thick enough to pipe.

Spoon the mixture into a piping bag fitted with a star nozzle and pipe whirls of truffle mixture into each tart case. Decorate with chocolate curls, made using a swivel vegetable peeler, dust with a little sifted icing sugar, if liked, and chill until ready to serve.

For chillied chocolate truffle tarts, melt 2 × 100 g (3½ oz) bars plain dark chocolate with chilli in the cream, then add 4 tablespoons rum instead of brandy. Chill, then pipe into the baked tarts as above.

baby banana & peach strudels

Makes **8**
Preparation time **30 minutes**
Cooking time **15–18 minutes**

2 **bananas**, about 175 g
  (6 oz) each with skin on,
  peeled and chopped
2 tablespoons **lemon juice**
2 small **ripe peaches**, about
  100 g (3½ oz) each, halved,
  stoned and sliced
100 g (3½ oz) **blueberries**
2 tablespoons **caster sugar**
2 tablespoons **fresh
  breadcrumbs**
½ teaspoon **ground
  cinnamo**n
6 sheets of **filo pastry**, each
  48 x 23 cm (19 x 9 inches)
  from a 270 g (8¾ oz) pack,
  defrosted if frozen
50 g (2 oz) **butter**, melted
sifted **icing sugar**, for dusting

Toss the bananas in the lemon juice, then place in a large bowl with the peach slices and blueberries. Mix the sugar, breadcrumbs and cinnamon in a small bowl, then gently mix with the fruit.

Unfold the pastry sheets and put one sheet on your work surface with the long edge facing you. Cut in half to make 2 x 23 x 25 cm (9 x 10 inch) rectangles. Put 2 heaped spoonfuls of the fruit mixture on each, then fold in the sides, brush the pastry with a little of the melted butter and roll up like a parcel. Repeat to make 8 mini strudels using 4 sheets of pastry.

Brush the strudels with a little more melted butter. Cut the remaining pastry sheets into wide strips, then wrap them like bandages around the strudels, covering any tears or splits in the pastry. Place on an ungreased baking sheet and brush with the remaining butter.

Bake in a preheated oven, 190°C (375°F), Gas Mark 5, for 15–18 minutes until golden brown and crisp. Leave to cool on the baking sheet, then dust with a little sifted icing sugar and arrange on a serving plate. These are best eaten on the day they are made.

For traditional apple strudels, replace the bananas and peaches with 500 g (1 lb) cored, peeled and sliced cooking apples tossed with 2 tablespoons lemon juice and mixed with 50 g (2 oz) sultanas. Replace the breadcrumbs with 2 tablespoons ground almonds and combine with the cinnamon. Increase the quantity of sugar to 50 g (2 oz) and continue the recipe as above.

lemon curd tarts

Makes **24**
Preparation time **40 minutes**,
    plus chilling and cooling
Cooking time **15 minutes**

1 quantity **pâte sucrée**
    (see page 11), chilled
2 **eggs**
200 g (7 oz) **caster sugar**
50 g (2 oz) **butter**, melted
grated rind of 1½ **lemons**,
    plus extra to decorate
4 tablespoons **lemon juice**
200 g (7 oz) **crème fraîche**

Roll the pastry out thinly on a lightly floured surface, then stamp out 24 × 6 cm (2½ inch) circles with a fluted biscuit cutter and press into the buttered sections of 2 × 12-section mini muffin tins. Reknead and reroll the pastry trimmings as needed. Prick the base of each tart 2–3 times with a fork, then chill for 15 minutes.

Beat the eggs and sugar together, then mix in the melted butter, lemon rind and juice. Spoon into the tart cases and bake in a preheated oven, 180°C (350°F), Gas Mark 4, for 15 minutes until just set. The tarts will be quite puffed up when you first take them out of the oven, but as they cool they will sink down again.

Leave to cool in the tins, then loosen the pastry with a knife, lift the tarts out of the tins and arrange on a serving plate. Top each with a small spoonful of crème fraîche and grated lemon rind to garnish.

For citrus curd tarts, make up the filling with the grated rind of ½ lemon, ½ lime and ½ orange and 4 tablespoons of mixed juice. Continue as above.

white chocolate & raspberry tarts

Makes **24**
Preparation time **30 minutes**,
  plus chilling and cooling
Cooking time **9–10 minutes**

1 quantity **pâte sucrée** (see
  page 11), chilled
150 g (5 oz) **white chocolate**,
  broken into pieces
300 ml (½ pint) **double cream**
2 tablespoons finely chopped
  mint
24 **raspberries**, about 100 g
  (3½ oz)
tiny **mint leaves**, to decorate
sifted **icing sugar**, for dusting

Roll the pastry out thinly on a lightly floured surface, then stamp out 24 × 6 cm (2½ inch) circles with a fluted biscuit cutter and press into the buttered sections of 2 × 12-section mini muffin tins. Reknead and reroll the pastry trimmings as needed. Prick the base of each tart 2–3 times with a fork, then chill for 15 minutes.

Line the tarts with small squares of nonstick baking paper and baking beans and bake in a preheated oven, 190°C (375°F), Gas Mark 5, for 5 minutes. Remove the paper and beans and cook for a further 4–5 minutes until the bases are crisp. Remove the cases from the tins and cool on a wire rack.

Melt the chocolate in a bowl over a saucepan of very gently simmering water, making sure that the base of the bowl does not touch the water. Stir until smooth.

Whip the cream until it forms soft swirls, then fold in the melted chocolate and chopped mint. Spoon into the cooled pastry cases and top each one with a raspberry and tiny mint leaf. Dust lightly with sifted icing sugar just before serving.

For dark chocolate & raspberry tarts, make up the pastry, replacing 15 g (½ oz) of the flour with 15 g (½ oz) cocoa powder. Fold 100 g (3½ oz) melted plain dark chocolate into the cream with 2 tablespoons icing sugar and the finely chopped mint. Decorate with raspberries, tiny mint leaves and a dusting of sifted icing sugar as above.

citrus baklava

Makes **24**
Preparation time **30 minutes**,
 plus chilling
Cooking time **35–40 minutes**

400 g (13 oz) **filo pastry**,
 defrosted if frozen
125 g (4 oz) **butter**, melted

For the filling
100 g (3½ oz) **walnut pieces**
100 g (3½ oz) **shelled
 pistachio nuts**
100 g (3½ oz) **blanched
 almonds**
75 g (3 oz) **caster sugar**
½ teaspoon **ground cinnamon**

For the syrup
1 **lemon**
1 small **orange**
250 g (8 oz) **caster sugar**
pinch of **ground cinnamon**
150 ml (¼ pint) **water**

To decorate
few slivers **pistachio nuts**

Dry-fry the nuts in a nonstick pan for 3–4 minutes, stirring until lightly browned. Leave to cool slightly then roughly chop and mix with the sugar and spice.

Unfold the pastry and cut it into rectangles the same size as the base of an 18 x 28 cm (7 x 11 inch) small roasting tin. Wrap half the pastry in clingfilm so that it doesn't dry out. Brush each unwrapped sheet of pastry with melted butter then layer up in the roasting tin. Spoon in the nut mixture then unwrap and cover with the remaining pastry, buttering layers as you go.

Cut the pastry into 6 squares, then cut each square into 4 triangles. Bake in a preheated oven, 180°C (350°F), Gas Mark 4, for 30–35 minutes, covering with foil after 20 minutes to prevent it overbrowning.

Meanwhile, make the syrup. Pare the rind off the citrus fruits with a zester or vegetable peeler then cut the rind into strips. Squeeze the juice. Put the strips and juice in a saucepan with the sugar, cinnamon and water. Heat gently until the sugar dissolves then simmer for 5 minutes without stirring.

Pour the hot syrup over the pastry as soon as it comes out of the oven. Leave to cool, then chill for 3 hours. Remove from the tin and arrange the pieces on a serving plate, sprinkled with slivers of pistachio. Store in the refrigerator for up to 2 days.

For rose water baklava, omit the orange rind and juice from the syrup and add 4 tablespoons extra water and 1 tablespoon rose water, or to taste. Pour over the cooked baklava and finish as above.

mini pine nut & honey tarts

Makes **24**
Preparation time **30 minutes**,
   plus chilling
Cooking time **17–20 minutes**

1 quantity **pâte sucrée** (see
   page 11), chilled
50 g (2 oz) **butter**, at room
   temperature
50 g (2 oz) **caster sugar**
3 tablespoons **thick-set
   honey**
grated rind of ½ **lemon**
1 **egg**
1 **egg yolk**
100 g (3½ oz) **pine nuts**
sifted **icing sugar**, for dusting
   (optional)

Roll the pastry out thinly on a lightly floured surface, then stamp out 24 × 6 cm (2½ inch) circles with a fluted biscuit cutter and press into the buttered sections of 2 × 12-section mini muffin tins. Reknead and reroll the pastry trimmings as needed. Prick the base of each tart 2–3 times with a fork, then chill for 15 minutes.

Line the tarts with small squares of nonstick baking paper and baking beans and bake in a preheated oven, 190°C (375°F), Gas Mark 5, for 5 minutes. Remove the paper and beans and cook for a further 4–5 minutes until the bases are crisp.

Cream the butter and sugar together, beat in the honey and lemon rind, then the egg and egg yolk. Reserve about one quarter of the pine nuts, then stir the rest into the honey mix.

Spoon into the baked tart cases and sprinkle with the remaining pine nuts. Bake for 8–10 minutes until golden and the filling is set. Leave to cool for 15 minutes, then remove from the tins and leave to cool on a wire rack. Dust with icing sugar, if liked.

For spiced walnut & honey tarts, make up the tart cases and filling as above, replacing the lemon rind and pine nuts with ¼ teaspoon ground cinnamon and 100 g (3½ oz) chopped walnuts.

blueberry tarts

Makes **24**
Preparation time **30 minutes**,
  plus chilling and cooling
Cooking time **11–13 minutes**

1 quantity of **orange-
  flavoured pâte sucrée** (see
  page 11), chilled
2 teaspoons **cornflour**
3 teaspoons **water**
40 g (1½ oz) **caster sugar**,
  plus extra for sprinkling
300 g (10 oz) **blueberries**
milk, to glaze

Roll the pastry out thinly on a lightly floured surface, then stamp out 24 × 6 cm (2½ inch) circles with a fluted biscuit cutter and press into the buttered sections of 2 × 12-section mini muffin tins, reserving any trimmings. Prick the base of each tart 2–3 times with a fork, then chill for 15 minutes.

Meanwhile, mix the cornflour and measurement water to a paste in a saucepan, then add the sugar and half the blueberries. Cook over a medium heat for 2–3 minutes until the blueberries soften and the juices begin to run. Take off the heat and add the remaining blueberries. Leave to cool.

Roll out the remaining pastry trimmings and cut out 24 tiny heart shapes. Place the heart shapes on a baking sheet, brush with milk and sprinkle with caster sugar.

Line the tarts with small squares of nonstick baking paper and baking beans and bake in a preheated oven, 190°C (375°F), Gas Mark 5, for 5 minutes. Remove the paper and beans from the tarts and cook for a further 4–5 minutes until the bases are crisp, cooking the heart shapes for 4–5 minutes on the shelf below.

Transfer the tart cases to a wire rack to cool. When ready to serve, spoon in the blueberry compote and top with the heart shapes.

For mini jam tarts, make up the tart cases and decorations as above. Spoon in 200 g (7 oz) strawberry jam, add the pastry shapes, then bake at 180°C (350°F), Gas Mark 4, for 12–15 minutes. Leave the tarts to cool for 5 minutes, then transfer to a wire rack to cool completely.

plum tripiti

Makes **24**
Preparation time **40 minutes**
Cooking time **10 minutes**

100 g (3½ oz) **feta cheese**,
   drained and coarsely grated
100 g (3½ oz) **ricotta cheese**
50 g (2 oz) **caster sugar**
¼ teaspoon **ground cinnamon**
1 **egg**, beaten
75 g (3 oz) **unsalted butter**
12 sheets chilled **filo pastry**
   from a 200 g (7 oz) pack
a little **flour**, for dusting
500 g (1 lb) small red **plums**,
   halved and pitted
icing sugar, for dusting

Mix the feta, ricotta, sugar, cinnamon and egg in a bowl. Melt the butter in a small saucepan.

Unfold the pastry sheets on a lightly floured surface, then put one in front of you, with a short side facing you. Cover the remaining sheets with clingfilm to prevent them drying out. Brush the pastry sheet with a little of the melted butter, then cut in half to make two long strips. Place a spoonful of the cheese mixture a little up from the bottom left-hand corner of each strip, then cover with a plum half. Fold the bottom right-hand corner of one strip diagonally over the plum to cover the filling and to make a triangle.

Fold the bottom left-hand corner upwards to make a second triangle, then keep folding until the top of the strip is reached and the filling is enclosed in a triangle of pastry. Place on a baking sheet and repeat until 24 triangles have been made using all the filling.

Brush the outside of the triangles with the remaining butter and cook in a preheated oven, 200°C (400°F), Gas Mark 6, for about 10 minutes until the pastry is golden and the plum juices begin to run from the sides. Dust with a little sifted icing sugar and leave to cool for 15 minutes before serving.

For gingered peach tripiti, make the filling in the same way but flavour with 2 tablespoons finely chopped glacé or stem ginger instead of ground cinnamon. Top with 2 ripe peaches, each cut into 12 pieces.

tiny treacle tarts

Makes **24**
Preparation time **30 minutes**,
    plus chilling
Cooking time **25 minutes**

1 quantity **pâte sucrée** (see
    page 11), chilled
50 g (2 oz) **butter**
75 g (3 oz) **light muscovado
    sugar**
300 g (10 oz) **golden syrup**
grated rind of **1 lemon**
2 tablespoons **lemon juice**
1 **egg**, beaten
50 g (2 oz) **fresh
    breadcrumbs**

Roll the pastry out thinly on a lightly floured surface, then stamp out 24 × 6 cm (2½ inch) circles with a fluted biscuit cutter and press into the buttered sections of 2 × 12-section mini muffin tins. Reknead and reroll pastry trimmings as needed. Chill for 15 minutes.

Put the butter, sugar, syrup, lemon rind and juice in a small saucepan and cook over a low heat until the butter has just melted and the sugar dissolved. Take off the heat and leave to cool slightly.

Stir the beaten egg and breadcrumbs into the syrup mix and beat until smooth. Spoon into the pastry cases.

Bake in a preheated oven, 180°C (350°F), Gas Mark 4, for 15–20 minutes. Leave to cool for 15 minutes, then loosen the tarts with a knife and remove from the tins. Transfer to a wire rack and leave to cool slightly. Serve warm with spoonfuls of whipped cream sprinkled with ground cinnamon.

For ginger & oat treacle tarts, add 1 teaspoon ground ginger to the syrup mix, then stir in the lemon rind and juice, beaten egg and 50 g (2 oz) porridge oats instead of the breadcrumbs. Cook as above.

potuguese custard tarts

Makes **12**

Preparation time **25 minutes**, plus cooling

Cooking time **35 minutes**

1 tablespoon **vanilla sugar**
½ teaspoon **ground cinnamon**
450 g (14½ oz) chilled ready-made or homemade **sweet shortcrust pastry** (see page 9)
a little **flour**, for dusting
3 **eggs**
2 **egg yolks**
2 tablespoons **caster sugar**
1 teaspoon **vanilla essence**
300 ml (½ pint) **double cream**
150 ml (¼ pint) **milk**
icing sugar, for dusting

Mix the vanilla sugar with the cinnamon. Cut the pastry in half and roll out each piece on a lightly floured surface to a 20 cm (8 inch) square. Sprinkle 1 square with the spiced sugar and position the second square on top. Reroll the pastry to a 40 x 30 cm (16 x 12 inch) rectangle and cut out 12 circles, each 10 cm (4 inches) across, using a large cutter or small bowl as a guide.

Press the pastry circles into the sections of a 12-hole nonstick muffin tray, pressing them firmly into the bottom and around the sides. Prick each pastry base, line with a square of foil, add macaroni or beans and bake blind (see page 15) in a preheated oven, 190°C (375°F), Gas Mark 5, for 10 minutes. Remove the foil and macaroni or beans and bake for an additional 5 minutes. Reduce the oven temperature to 160°C (325°F), Gas Mark 3.

Beat together the eggs, egg yolks, caster sugar and vanilla essence. Heat the cream and milk in a pan until bubbling around the edges and pour it over the egg mixture, stirring. Strain the custard into a jug and pour into the pastry shells.

Bake for about 20 minutes or until the custard is only just set. Let the tarts cool in the tin, then remove and serve dusted with icing sugar.

For French prune custard tarts, put 12 ready-to-eat pitted prunes in the base of each blind-baked pastry case, then pour the custard over and bake as above. Serve warm with spoonfuls of crème fraîche.

savoury
light bites

smoked salmon & mint pea tarts

Makes **6**
Preparation time **20 minutes**
Cooking time **15 minutes**

500 g (1 lb) **ready-made puff
pastry**, defrosted if frozen
25 g (1 oz) **butter**
6 **spring onions**, thinly sliced
250 g (8 oz) **frozen peas**,
defrosted
2 **Little Gem lettuces**, thickly
sliced
2 tablespoons chopped **mint**
250 g (8 oz) **full-fat crème
fraîche**
200 g (7 oz) **smoked salmon**
salt and **pepper**

Cut the pastry into 6 pieces, then roll each piece out
on a lightly floured surface and trim to a 15 cm (6 inch)
circle using a saucer as a guide. Transfer to 2 large,
lightly oiled baking sheets. Mark smaller circles 2.5 cm
(1 inch) in from the edges, then prick all over the inner
circles with a fork.

Bake in a preheated oven, 200°C (400°F), Gas Mark 6,
for 10 minutes until well risen. Press down the centre
with a fork and cook for a further 5 minutes until the
tart cases are crisp and golden.

When the tart cases are almost ready, heat the butter
in a frying pan, then add the spring onions and fry until
softened. Add the peas and cook for a few minutes
until hot, add the lettuce and cook for 30 seconds,
then stir in the mint, crème fraîche and salt and pepper.

Spoon the pea mixture into the hot tart cases and
arrange the smoked salmon in folds on top. Sprinkle
with a little extra pepper and serve at once with salad.

For bacon, pea & spinach tarts, make up the tart
cases as above. Fry the spring onions in butter, add
the peas and 150 g (5 oz) spinach and cook until
just wilted. Stir in the crème fraîche, 1 teaspoon
wholegrain mustard, salt and pepper, then spoon into
the tart cases and top with 6 grilled and diced back
bacon rashers.

mexican egg tarts

Makes **4**

Preparation time **25 minutes**,
plus chilling

Cooking time **25–28 minutes**

1 quantity **shortcrust pastry**
(see page 9)

1 tablespoon **olive oil**

1 **onion**, chopped

1 **red pepper**, cored,
deseeded and diced

75 g (3 oz) **ready-diced
chorizo sausage**

2 **garlic cloves**, finely
chopped

¼ teaspoon **smoked paprika**

2 **bay leaves**

200 g (7 oz) can **chopped
tomatoes**

150 g (5 oz) **cherry tomatoes**,
halved

4 **eggs**

salt and **pepper**

a few **tiny basil leaves**,
optional

grated **Cheddar cheese**, to
serve

Cut the pastry into 4 pieces, then roll each piece out on a lightly floured surface until a little larger than a buttered 12 cm (5 inch) fluted loose-bottomed tart tin. Lift the pastry into the tins, then press over the base and sides. Trim off the excess pastry with scissors a little above the top of the tin. Prick the bases with a fork, then put on a baking sheet. Chill for 15 minutes.

Heat the oil in a saucepan, add the onion, red pepper and chorizo and fry for 5 minutes until softened. Stir in the garlic, paprika and bay leaves, then add the canned tomatoes and season with salt and pepper. Simmer gently, uncovered for 15 minutes, stirring from time to time until thickened. Discard the bay leaves.

Meanwhile bake the tarts blind (see page 15) for 8 minutes. Remove the paper and beans and cook for a further 4 minutes until golden.

Stir the cherry tomatoes into the hot sauce and spoon into the hot pastry cases. Make a dip in the centre, then break an egg into each. Sprinkle with salt and pepper and cook for 5–8 minutes until the egg is to your liking.

Remove the tarts from the tins, transfer to serving plates, sprinkle with basil leaves, if liked, grated cheese and serve with a three bean salad.

For creamy spinach & egg tarts, heat 15 g (½ oz) butter in a frying pan, add 150 g (5 oz) spinach and cook until just wilted. Mix with 2 tablespoons double cream, a little grated nutmeg, salt and pepper. Spoon into the hot tart cases, make a dip in the centre, break an egg into each, then bake as above and sprinkle with grated cheese just before serving.

spinach & pine nut tarts

Makes **6**
Preparation time **25 minutes**,
  plus chilling
Cooking time **27–28 minutes**

1 quantity **shortcrust pastry**
  (see page 9)
250 g (8 oz) **spinach**
25 g (1 oz) **butter**
1 small **onion**, finely chopped
2 **garlic cloves**, finely
  chopped
¼ teaspoon **grated nutmeg**
3 **eggs**
250 ml (8 fl oz) **crème fraîche**
3 tablespoons **pine nuts**
salt and **pepper**

Roll the pastry out thinly on a lightly floured surface and use to line 6 buttered 10 cm (4 inch) fluted loose-bottomed tart tins, rekneading and rerolling the pastry trimmings as needed. Trim off the excess pastry from the top of each tart with scissors so that it stands a little above the tin. Put on a baking sheet and chill for 15 minutes.

Rinse the spinach well, drain in a colander, then dry-fry with just the water clinging to the leaves for 2–3 minutes until the leaves have just wilted. Scoop out of the pan with a slotted spoon, pressing out any excess moisture, then finely chop the leaves.

Drain and dry the pan, then heat the butter and fry the onion for 5 minutes until softened. Stir in the garlic, cook briefly, then return the spinach to the pan. Season with nutmeg and salt and pepper.

Beat the eggs in a bowl, add the crème fraîche and mix until smooth, then mix with the spinach. Divide between the tarts and sprinkle with the pine nuts.

Bake in a preheated oven, 180°C (350°F), Gas Mark 4, for 20 minutes until the filling is set and the pine nuts are golden. Check after 15 minutes and cover the tops of the tarts loosely with foil if they seem to be browning too quickly. Leave to cool for 5 minutes, then remove from the tins and serve with a green salad.

For spinach & Stilton tarts, make up the tart cases and filling as above, but mix the eggs with 250 ml (8 fl oz) milk and 150 g (5 oz) crumbled Stilton instead of the crème fraîche and nutmeg, and bake the tarts without the pine nut topping.

chillied pumpkin & tomato pies

Makes **4**
Preparation time **30 minutes**
Cooking time **40–45 minutes**

1 tablespoon **olive oil**
1 large **red onion**, chopped
400 g (13 oz) deseeded
   **pumpkin (or butternut
   squash** if out of season),
   peeled, cut into small dice
2 cloves **garlic**, finely chopped
½ teaspoon **smoked paprika**
400 g (13 oz) can **chopped
   tomatoes**
1 quantity **shortcrust pastry**
   (see page 9)
100 g (3½ oz) **feta cheese**,
   drained, crumbled
beaten egg, to glaze
salt and **pepper**

Heat the oil in a saucepan, add the onion and pumpkin and fry for 5 minutes until softened. Stir in the garlic and paprika, then the tomatoes and a little salt and pepper. Cover and simmer for 15 minutes, stirring from time to time until the pumpkin is just cooked.

Cut the pastry into 4 pieces then roll each piece out on a lightly floured surface until large enough to line a buttered 12 cm (5 inch) fluted loose-bottomed tart tin. Press over the base and sides, then trim the top level with the tin. Reserve the pastry trimmings.

Put the tarts on a baking sheet, spoon in the pumpkin filling, then sprinkle with crumbled feta. Brush the top edge of the pastry with a little beaten egg. Roll out the pastry trimmings and cut into narrow strips, long enough to go over the tops of the pies. Arrange as a lattice on each pie, then brush with a little egg.

Bake in a preheated oven, 180°C (350°F), Gas Mark 4, for 20–25 minutes until golden brown. Leave to stand for 5 minutes, then remove from the tins and serve warm or cold.

For chillied pumpkin & bacon pies, make up the filling and tart cases as above, omitting the feta, and adding 4 grilled back bacon rashers, diced and mixed into the filling. Add the pastry lattice and bake as above.

pizza puff pies

Makes **6**
Preparation time **25 minutes**
Cooking time **40 minutes**

1 tablespoon **olive oil**
1 **onion**, chopped
1 **garlic clove**, finely chopped
400 g (13 oz) can **chopped tomatoes**
1 teaspoon **caster sugar**
500 g (1 lb) **ready-made puff pastry**, defrosted if frozen
small bunch of **basil**
125 g (4 oz) pack **mozzarella cheese**, drained
6 **pitted black olives** (optional)
salt and **pepper**
olive oil, to serve (optional)

Heat the oil in a saucepan, add the onion and fry for 5 minutes until softened. Add the garlic, tomatoes and sugar, and season with salt and pepper. Cover and simmer gently for 15 minutes, stirring from time to time until the sauce has thickened. Leave to cool slightly.

Cut the pastry into 6, then roll out each piece on a lightly floured surface and trim to a 15 cm (6 inch) circle using a saucer as a guide. Press each pastry circle into the base of a lightly oiled metal Yorkshire pudding tin or tart tin, 10 cm (4 inches) in diameter, 2.5 cm (1 inch) deep, and press the pastry at intervals to the sides of the tin to give a wavy edge.

Reserve half the smaller basil leaves for garnish, tear the larger leaves into pieces and stir into the sauce. Divide the sauce between the pies and spread into an even layer. Cut the mozzarella into 6 slices and add a slice to each pie. Sprinkle the mozzarella with a little salt and pepper, and add an olive to each, if using.

Bake in a preheated oven, 200°C (400°F), Gas Mark 6, for 20 minutes until the pastry is crisp and golden. Leave to cool for 5 minutes, then turn out. Drizzle with a little olive oil, if liked, sprinkle with remaining basil leaves and serve warm with salad.

For mushroom & anchovy puff pies, add 125 g (4 oz) sliced button mushrooms to the tomato sauce for the last 5 minutes of cooking. Spoon the sauce into the pies, top with mozzarella, then omit the olives. Halve 6 anchovy fillets from a 50 g (2 oz) can, arrange two halves as a cross on top of each pie, then bake and garnish as above.

french onion tarts

Makes **12**
Preparation time **30 minutes**,
    plus chilling
Cooking time **30–35 minutes**

1 quantity **all-butter
    shortcrust pastry** (see
    page 9)
50 g (2 oz) **butter**
2 **onions**, thinly sliced
4 **eggs**
200 ml (7 fl oz) **milk**
2 teaspoons **Dijon mustard**
125 g (4 oz) **Gruyère cheese**,
    finely grated
salt and **pepper**

Roll the pastry out thinly on a lightly floured surface, then stamp out 12 x 10 cm (4 inch) circles, with a plain biscuit cutter, and press into a buttered 12-section muffin tin. Reknead and reroll the pastry trimmings as needed. Chill for 15 minutes.

Heat the butter in a frying pan, add the onions and fry over a gentle heat for 10 minutes, stirring from time to time until softened and just beginning to colour.

Add the eggs, milk and mustard to a large wide-necked jug, and fork together until just mixed. Add the cheese and seasoning and mix together. Divide the mixture between the pastry cases, then spoon in the fried onions.

Bake in a preheated oven, 190°C (375°F), Gas Mark 5, for 20–25 minutes until golden brown and the filling is just set. Leave to cool for 10 minutes, then loosen the edges of the tarts with a knife and remove from the tins. Serve warm or cold with salad.

For onion & chorizo tarts, heat 25 g (1 oz) butter in a frying pan, add 1 sliced onion and 100 g (3½ oz) diced chorizo sausage and fry until the onions are softened and just beginning to brown. Fork 4 eggs, 200 ml (7 fl oz) milk, 125 g (4 oz) grated Gruyère, a few fresh thyme leaves and salt and pepper together. Add the custard, then the onion and chorizo mix, to the pastry cases and cook as above.

salmon & courgette tarts

Makes **4**
Preparation time **30 minutes**,
  plus chilling
Cooking time **30–40 minutes**

1 quantity **all-butter
  shortcrust pastry** (see
  page 9)
2 × 150 g (5 oz) **salmon
  steaks**
25 g (1 oz) **butter**
4 **spring onions**, thinly sliced
1 small **courgette**, diced
2 **eggs**
150 ml (¼ pint) **milk**
2 teaspoons finely chopped
  tarragon
50 g (2 oz) **Cheddar cheese**,
  grated
salt and **pepper**

Cut the pastry into 4 pieces, then roll each piece out on a lightly floured surface until large enough to line the base and sides of a buttered 12 cm (5 inch) fluted loose-bottomed tart tin. Lift the pastry into the tins, press over the base and sides, then trim the top of the pastry with scissors so its stands a little above the top of the tins. Put on a baking sheet and chill for 15 minutes while making the filling.

Put the salmon in the top of a steamer, cover and cook for 8–10 minutes until the salmon can be broken into flakes easily and the flakes are pale pink all the way through. Lift out and put on to a plate, remove the skin (if there is any) and break into flakes, checking for and removing any bones.

Heat the butter in a small frying pan, add the spring onions and courgette and fry gently for 3–4 minutes until softened. Beat the eggs, milk and tarragon together with a little salt and pepper, then stir in the cheese.

Pour the egg mixture into the tarts, add the flaked fish, onion and courgette mix and bake in a preheated oven, 190°C (375°F), Gas Mark 5, for 20–25 minutes until golden and the filling is just set. Serve warm or cold.

For creamy prawn & crab tarts, fry 1 small onion in 25 g (1 oz) butter until softened. Add 2 deseeded and diced tomatoes and cook for 2 minutes. Beat 2 eggs with 150 ml (1/4 pint) double cream and milk mixed, 50 g (2 oz) grated Cheddar, salt, cayenne pepper and a 40 g (1½ oz) can dark crab meat. Pour into the tart cases, then add 150 g (5 oz) cooked peeled prawns, defrosted if frozen. Bake as above.

creamy mushroom & stilton pies

Makes **8**
Preparation time **30 minutes**,
  plus cooling
Cooking time **25 minutes**

25 g (1 oz) **butter**
1 tablespoon **olive oil**
1 **onion**, finely chopped
250 g (8 oz) mixed
  mushrooms, sliced
2 **garlic cloves**, finely
  chopped
3 sprigs **thyme**, leaves torn
  from stems
500 g (1 lb) **ready-made puff
  pastry**, defrosted if frozen
120 ml (4 fl oz) **full-fat crème
  fraîche**
175 g (6 oz) **Stilton cheese**,
  diced with rind removed
beaten egg, to glaze
salt and **pepper**

Heat the butter and oil in a frying pan, add the onion and fry for a few minutes until just beginning to soften, then add the mushrooms and garlic and fry, stirring until golden. Take off the heat, add the thyme leaves and leave to cool.

Roll the pastry out thinly on a lightly floured surface and trim to a 35 cm (14 inch) square, then cut into 16 squares. Spoon the mushroom mixture over the centre of 8 of the squares, then top with crème fraîche and cheese. Brush the edges of the pastry with egg, then cover each with a second pastry square.

Press the edges of the pastry together well and crimp the edges, if liked. Transfer to a baking sheet, then slash the tops with a knife, brush with beaten egg and sprinkle with salt flakes and extra thyme, if liked. Bake in a preheated oven, 200°C (400°F), Gas Mark 6, for 20 minutes until well risen and golden brown. Serve warm with salad.

For devilled mushroom pies, add 250 g (8 oz) sliced cup mushrooms to the fried onion as above, fry until golden, then add 1 teaspoon Worcestershire sauce, 1 teaspoon English mustard, 1 teaspoon tomato purée and 2 chopped tomatoes. Fry for a few minutes until the tomatoes are softened, then cool and add to the pastry squares as above.

caribbean chicken patties

Makes **4**
Preparation time **30 minutes**,
 plus chilling
Cooking time **30–35 minutes**

2 tablespoons **sunflower oil**
250 g (8 oz) boneless, skinless
 chicken breast, diced
250 g (8 oz) **butternut
 squash**, deseeded, peeled
 and cut into small dice
1 small **onion**, chopped
2 **garlic cloves**, finely
 chopped
½ small **hot bonnet chilli**,
 deseeded and finely chopped
1 **red** or **orange pepper**,
 deseeded and diced
1 teaspoon **mild curry
 powder** or **paste**
2 tablespoons chopped
 coriander
beaten egg, to glaze
pepper

For the pastry
250 g (8 oz) **plain flour**
1½ teaspoons **turmeric**
125 g (4 oz) **white vegetable
 fat**, diced
2½–3 tablespoons **cold water**
salt

Make the pastry. Add flour, turmeric, a little salt and the fat to a mixing bowl, and rub the fat in with your fingertips or using an electric mixer until you have fine crumbs. Gradually mix in enough of the measurement water to form a soft but not sticky dough. Knead lightly, then wrap in clingfilm and chill while making the filling.

Heat the oil in a frying pan, add the chicken and butternut squash and fry for 5 minutes until the chicken is just beginning to brown. Add the onion, garlic, chilli and pepper and fry for 5 minutes until the vegetables are softened and the chicken cooked through. Add the curry powder, coriander and a little pepper and cook briefly, then take off the heat and leave to cool.

Cut the pastry into 4 pieces, roll each piece out on a lightly floured surface and trim to an 18 cm (7 inch) circle. Divide the filling between the pastry circles, brush the edges with beaten egg, then fold in half and press the edges together well, first with your fingertips, then with the prongs of a fork, until well sealed.

Transfer to an oiled baking sheet, brush the patties with beaten egg and bake in a preheated oven, 190°C (375°F), Gas Mark 5, for 20–25 minutes. Serve hot or cold with chilli tomato chutney.

For cheesy chilli patties, omit the chicken when frying the butternut squash. Omit the curry powder and add 100 g (3½ oz) frozen sweetcorn, defrosted, and 100 g (3½ oz) diced Red Leicester cheese when adding the coriander, but to cooled filling, rather than hot.

savoyarde potato pies

Makes **4**
Preparation time **30 minutes**
Cooking time **35–45 minutes**

500 g (1 lb) **new potatoes,**
   scrubbed and thinly sliced
25 g (1 oz) **butter**
3 **shallots,** thinly sliced, plus
   1 large **shallot,** cut into
   4 thick slices
3 **garlic cloves,** finely
   chopped
250 ml (8 fl oz) **double cream**
1 **egg yolk**
2 tablespoons chopped
   chives
2 teaspoons chopped **thyme,**
   plus extra leaves to decorate
¼ teaspoon **grated nutmeg**
500 g (1 lb) **ready-made puff
   pastry,** defrosted if frozen
100 g (3½ oz) **Emmental
   cheese,** grated
beaten egg, to glaze
1 large **shallot,** cut into 4 thick
   slices
salt and **pepper**

Add the potatoes to a large saucepan of boiling water, bring back to the boil, then cook for 3–4 minutes until only just tender. Tip into a colander and drain well.

Heat the butter in a frying pan, add the shallots and garlic and fry for 4–5 minutes until softened and just turning golden. Fork the cream, egg yolk, herbs, nutmeg and a generous amount of salt and pepper together.

Cut the pastry into 4 then roll out each piece thinly on a lightly floured surface to a rough 20 cm (8 inch) circle. Use to line 4 buttered individual 10 cm (4 inch) springform tins, leaving the excess pastry hanging over the sides.

Divide half the potatoes between the tins, top with the fried shallots, cheese and the rest of the potatoes. Cover with the cream mix, squeeze the ends of the pastry together to enclose the filling, trimming off any excess, and brush the edges with beaten egg to stick together.

Brush the tops with beaten egg, add a slice of shallot on top and sprinkle with thyme leaves, salt and pepper. Bake in a preheated oven, 200°C (400°F), Gas Mark 6, for 30–35 minutes. Check after 20 minutes and cover with foil if the pastry is browning too quickly.

Stand for 5 minutes, loosen the edges with a knife, remove the tins and serve hot with a rocket and bacon salad.

For mustard potato & pastrami pie, make up the pies as above, omitting the herbs and adding 2 teaspoons wholegrain mustard instead. Layer the sliced potatoes and onion with 100 g (3½ oz) sliced pastrami instead of the cheese. Top with the rest of the potatoes, then the mustard cream mix. Continue as above.

mini raised chicken & chorizo pies

Makes **6**
Preparation time **40 minutes**,
  plus cooling
Cooking time **45 minutes**

300 g (10 oz) good-quality
  pork sausagemeat
250 g (8 oz) **mini chicken
  breast fillets**, diced
125 g (4 oz) **chorizo
  sausage**, diced
50 g (2 oz) **sun-dried
  tomatoes in olive oil**,
  drained and chopped
6 **spring onions**, chopped
2 tablespoons chopped
  rosemary leaves
milk, to glaze
salt and **cayenne pepper**
coarse sea salt and **paprika**
  to decorate (optional)

For the hot water crust pastry
175 g (6 oz) **lard**
175 ml (6 fl oz) **milk** and
  water, mixed half and half
375 g (12 oz) **plain flour**
¼ teaspoon **salt**
¼ teaspoon **cayenne pepper**

Make the hot water crust pastry as on page 11, adding the cayenne pepper with the flour and salt. Leave to cool for 10–20 minutes while making the filling.

Mix the sausagemeat, chicken and chorizo together, then add the sun-dried tomatoes, spring onions and rosemary. Season generously with salt and cayenne pepper.

Reserve one-third of the pastry, then cut the remainder into 6 pieces. Press one piece over the base and sides of an ungreased individual springform tin, 10 cm (4 inches) in diameter and 4.5 cm (1¾ inches) deep. Repeat with the remaining portions of pastry until 6 tins have been lined.

Divide the filling between the pies and press into an even layer. Cut the reserved pastry into 6 and roll out on a lightly floured surface into circles the same size as the tins. Place on top and press the edges together to seal.

Flute the edges (see page 17). Make 4 tiny steam vents in the top of the pies, then brush with milk and sprinkle with sea salt and paprika, if liked.

Bake in a preheated oven, 180°C (350°F), Gas Mark 4, for 45 minutes until golden brown and the filling is cooked. Check after 30 minutes and cover the tops loosely with foil if they seem to be browning too quickly. Cool for at least 30 minutes, then loosen the edges with a knife and remove the tins. Transfer to a wire rack and leave to cool completely.

For mini raised chicken & chutney pies, omit the chorizo and sun-dried tomatoes, adding 125 g (4 oz) diced back bacon. Press half the filling into the pie cases, spoon 3 tablespoons chutney between the pies, then top with the remaining filling and pastry lids as above.

stilton & leek tartlets

Serves **4**
Preparation time **15 minutes**
Cooking time **25 minutes**

1 teaspoon **olive oil**
8 small **leeks**, trimmed and
　finely sliced
50 g (2 oz) **Stilton cheese**,
　crumbled
1 teaspoon chopped **thyme**
2 **eggs**, beaten
4 tablespoons **low-fat crème**
　fraîche
12 x 15 cm (6 inch) squares
　of **filo pastry**
milk, for brushing

Heat the oil in a saucepan, add the leeks and fry for 3–4 minutes until softened.

Stir half the Stilton and the thyme into the leek mixture, then blend together the remaining Stilton, the eggs and crème fraîche in a bowl.

Brush the filo squares with a little milk and use them to line 4 fluted tins, each 10 cm (4 inches) in diameter. Spoon the leek mixture into the tins, then pour over the cheese and egg mixture.

Put the tins on a baking sheet and bake in a preheated oven, 200°C (400°F), Gas Mark 6, for 15–20 minutes until the filling is set, then serve.

For spring onion & Cheddar tartlets, use the same quantity of mature Cheddar cheese instead of Stilton and grate it coarsely. Slice 2 bunches of large spring onions instead of the leeks and fry for 1 minute, then remove from the heat. Add the spring onions to the cheese mixture and continue as above.

turkey & cranberry turnovers

Makes **6**
Preparation time **25 minutes**
Cooking time **20 minutes**

1 tablespoon **sunflower oil**
1 **onion**, chopped
250 g (8 oz) **minced turkey**
4 **smoked streaky bacon
  rashers**, diced
½ teaspoon **dried mixed
  herbs**
500 g (1 lb) **ready-made puff
  pastry**, defrosted if frozen
3 tablespoons **cranberry
  sauce**
beaten egg, to glaze
salt and **pepper**

Heat the oil in a frying pan, add the onion, turkey and bacon and fry, stirring, for 5 minutes until golden. Take off the heat and stir in the dried herbs and salt and pepper. Leave to cool.

Roll the pastry out thinly on a lightly floured surface and trim to a 25 × 50 cm (10 × 20 inch) rectangle, then cut into 8 × 12 cm (5 inch) squares. Divide the turkey mixture between the squares, top each with a little cranberry sauce, then brush the edges of the pastry with beaten egg.

Fold each pastry square in half to make a triangle, press the edges together well, then slash the tops with criss-cross lines. Transfer to a baking sheet, then brush with beaten egg and bake in a preheated oven, 200°C (400°F), Gas Mark 6, for 15–20 minutes until well risen and golden. Serve hot or cold.

For chicken & chutney turnovers, add 250 g (8 oz) diced mini chicken fillets to the fried onion and bacon, cook until golden, then mix with the dried herbs and seasoning. Add to the pastry squares and top with 3 tablespoons tomato chutney.

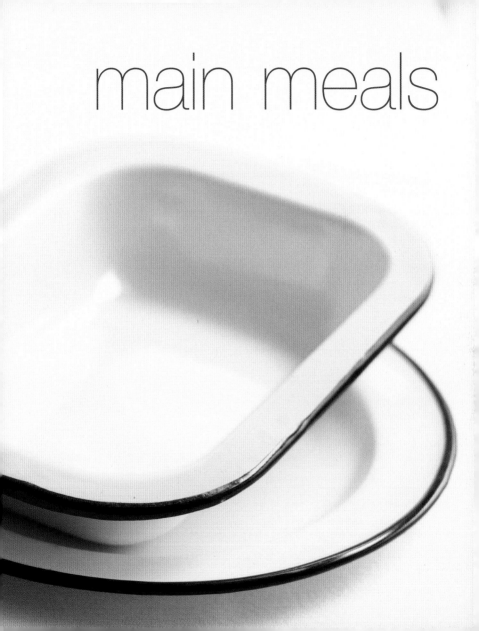

main meals

mediterranean vegetable pie

Serves **4**
Preparation time **30 minutes**
Cooking time **60–65 minutes**

2 large **aubergines**, sliced
5 tablespoons **olive oil**
1 large **red onion**, chopped
3 **garlic cloves**, finely chopped
400 g (13 oz) can **chopped
  tomatoes**
125 ml (4 fl oz) **red wine**
1 teaspoon **caster sugar**
4 teaspoons finely chopped
  rosemary leaves
2 **roasted red peppers** from a
  jar, drained and quartered
beaten egg, to glaze
salt and **pepper**

For the Parmesan pastry
375 g (12 oz) **plain flour**
175 g (6 oz) mixed **butter** and
  white vegetable fat, diced
50 g (2 oz) **Parmesan cheese**,
  grated, plus extra for
  sprinkling
2 tablespoons finely chopped
  rosemary leaves, plus extra
  for sprinkling
4–4½ tablespoons **cold water**
salt

Arrange the sliced aubergines on a foil-lined grill rack, drizzle with 2 tablespoons oil and sprinkle with salt and pepper. Grill for 5 minutes until browned, turn over, oil and season again, grill for a further 5 minutes, then set aside.

Heat the remaining oil in a saucepan, add the onion and fry for 5 minutes until softened. Add the garlic, tomatoes, wine, sugar and rosemary, then season well with salt and pepper. Simmer, uncovered, for 15 minutes, stirring from time to time until thickened, then leave to cool.

Make the pastry. Add the flour and a pinch of salt to a bowl, then rub in the fats with your fingertips or an electric mixer until you have fine crumbs. Stir in the Parmesan and rosemary, then mix in enough of the water to form a soft but not sticky dough. Knead lightly, then cut in half.

Roll one pastry half out thinly on a lightly floured board until large enough to cover a buttered 25 cm (10 inch) metal pie plate. Lift the pastry into the pie plate, then spoon one-third of the tomato sauce over the base. Arrange half the aubergines on top, cover with half the remaining sauce, then the red peppers. Repeat with the remaining aubergines and sauce.

Roll out the remaining pastry to form a lid. Brush the edge of the pastry on the plate with beaten egg. Lift the pastry over the pie, press the edges together and trim off any excess. Brush the top of the pie with egg, and sprinkle with rosemary and a little extra Parmesan.

Bake in a preheated oven, 190°C (375°F), Gas Mark 5, for 30–35 minutes until golden. Check after 20 minutes and cover with foil if needed. Serve hot cut into wedges.

picnic pie

Serves **6–8**
Preparation time **35 minutes**
Cooking time **1½ hours**

500 g (1 lb) lean **pork and leek** or **Cumberland sausages**, skinned
500 g (1 lb) boneless, skinless **chicken thighs**, chopped
125 g (4 oz) **smoked bacon**, diced
5 **cloves**, roughly crushed
¼ teaspoon **ground allspice**
small bunch of **sage**
1 **Braeburn apple**, cored and sliced
1 **egg yolk** mixed with 1 tablespoon **water**
salt and **pepper**

For the hot water crust pastry
175 g (6 oz) **lard**
175 ml (6 fl oz) **milk** and **water**, mixed half and half
2 teaspoons **English mustard**
375 g (12 oz) **plain flour**
¼ teaspoon **salt**

Make the hot water crust pastry according to the method on page 11, stirring the mustard into the melted lard mixture. Cool for 10 minutes.

Mix the sausagemeat, chicken, bacon, cloves, allspice and plenty of salt and pepper together in a bowl.

Reserve one-third of the pastry, press the remaining warm pastry over the base and sides of a deep 18 cm (7 inch) loose-bottomed cake tin. Spoon in half the meat filling and level. Cover with half the sage leaves, then the apple slices, then spoon over the rest of the filling. Level and top with the remaining sage. Brush the edges of the pastry with the egg glaze.

Roll out the reserved pastry to a circle a little larger than the tin, arrange on the pie and press the edges together. Trim off the excess, then crimp the edge. Roll out the trimmings and decorate (see page 17). Make a slit in the top of the pie, then brush with the egg glaze. Cook in a preheated oven, 180°C (350°F), Gas Mark 4, for 1½ hours, covering with foil after 40 minutes, when golden. Leave to cool then remove the tin. Put the pie, still on the tin base, in the refrigerator for 3–4 hours or overnight. When ready to serve, remove the base and cut the pie into wedges.

For apricot & pickled onion pie, make up the filling as above, but omit the sage and apples and replace with 100 g (3½ oz) sliced ready-to-eat dried apricots and 100 g (3½ oz) drained and sliced pickled onions.

salmon & asparagus en croûte

Serves **4**
Preparation time **25 minutes**
Cooking time **40–45 minutes**

25 g (1 oz) **butter**
175 g (6 oz) **asparagus**,
  trimmed
600–625 g (1lb 2oz–1lb 4 oz)
  salmon fillet, about
  18–20 cm (7–8 inches)
  long, skinned
juice of ½ **lemon**
500 g (1 lb) **ready-made puff
  pastry**, defrosted if frozen
100 g (3½ oz) **medium-fat
  soft cheese**
grated rind of **1 lemon**
1 tablespoon chopped
  tarragon
2 tablespoons chopped
  parsley
1½ teaspoons **green
  peppercorns**, drained and
  chopped (optional)
50 g (2 oz) **sunblush
  tomatoes**, drained and
  roughly chopped
beaten egg, to glaze
salt flakes, for sprinkling
salt and **pepper**

Heat the butter in a frying pan, add the asparagus and fry for 2–3 minutes until just softened, then season with salt and pepper. Drizzle the salmon with lemon juice and season.

Roll the pastry out thinly on a lightly floured surface and trim to a 35 cm (14 inch) square, then trim a 3.5 cm (1½ inch) strip off one of the sides. Put the salmon on top so that the long side of the salmon is parallel with the narrower side of the pastry rectangle.

Dot the cheese on top of the salmon, then sprinkle with the lemon rind, herbs, peppercorns if using, and tomatoes. Arrange the asparagus on top, alternating their direction.

Brush the pastry around the salmon with beaten egg, then fold the narrower sides up and over the salmon, pressing to seal. Cut the excess from the top ends of pastry, then fold and press to wrap the salmon like a parcel.

Brush the parcel with beaten egg and transfer to a baking sheet. Decorate (see page 16), and sprinkle with salt flakes, if liked. Bake in a preheated oven, 200°C (400°F), Gas Mark 6, for 35–40 minutes. Check after 25 minutes and cover with foil if the pastry seems to be browning too quickly. To test if the salmon is cooked, insert a knife into the centre, wait 3 seconds, then remove; if the knife feels hot it is cooked. Cut into thick slices and serve with lemon wedges.

For salmon & watercress en croûte, add 1 torn bunch of watercress to a food processor with the cheese, grated lemon rind and a little salt and pepper, and blitz until smooth. Spread over the salmon fillet on the pastry, then wrap the pastry around as above.

chicken & mushroom pies

Makes **4**
Preparation time **35 minutes**,
 plus chilling
Cooking time **1 hour**
 10 minutes

1 tablespoon **olive oil**
8 boneless, skinless **chicken
 thighs**, about 625 g (1¼ lb),
 cubed
1 **onion**, chopped
2 **garlic cloves**, finely
 chopped
2 tablespoons **plain flour**
150 ml (¼ pint) **white wine**
200 ml (7 fl oz) **chicken stock**
few sprigs **thyme** or a little
 dried thyme
25 g (1 oz) **butter**
125 g (4 oz) **closed-cup
 mushrooms**, sliced
beaten egg, to glaze
salt and **pepper**

For the pastry
300 g (10 oz) **plain flour**
1½ teaspoons **dry mustard
 powder**
150 g (5 oz) mixed **butter** and
 white vegetable fat, diced
3 tablespoons **cold water**
salt and **pepper**

Heat the oil in a large frying pan and fry the chicken, stirring, until beginning to colour. Add the onion and fry until the chicken is golden and the onion softened. Stir in the garlic, then mix in the flour. Add the wine, stock, thyme and a generous sprinkle of salt and pepper. Bring to the boil, stirring, then cover and simmer for 30 minutes.

Heat the butter in a small frying pan, add the mushrooms and fry until golden. Add to the chicken and leave to cool.

Make the pastry. Add the flour, mustard and a little salt and pepper to a mixing bowl. Add the fats and rub in using your fingertips or using an electric mixer until you have fine crumbs. Gradually mix in enough of the water to form a soft but not sticky dough. Knead lightly, wrap in clingfilm and chill for 15 minutes.

Reserve one-third of the pastry, then cut the rest into 4 pieces. Roll each piece out thinly, then line 4 buttered individual springform tins, 10 cm (4 inches) in diameter and 4.5 cm (1¾ inches) deep. Roll out the reserved pastry thinly and cut out lids, using the tins as a guide.

Spoon the chicken filling into the pies, brush the top edges with beaten egg, then add the lids and press the pastry edges together. Flute the edges and bake on a baking sheet in a preheated oven, 190°C (375°C), Gas Mark 5, for 30 minutes until golden. Leave to stand for 5 minutes, then loosen the edges, transfer to a plate and remove the tins. Serve with green vegetables.

For chicken & bacon pies, reduce the amount of chicken to 500 g (1 lb) and add 125 g (4 oz) diced streaky bacon when frying the chicken and onion.

summer prawn & fish filo pie

Serves **4**
Preparation time **10 minutes**
Cooking time **20–25 minutes**

750 g (1½ lb) **skinless white fish fillets**
100 g (3½ oz) **frozen cooked peeled prawns**, defrosted
100 g (3½ oz) **frozen peas**, defrosted
grated rind and juice of **1 lemon**
600 ml (1 pint) **ready-made white sauce**
1 bunch of **dill**, chopped
8 sheets of **filo pastry**
melted butter, for brushing
salt and **pepper**

Cut the fish into large, bite-sized pieces and put in a bowl with the prawns and peas. Add the lemon rind and juice, stir in the white sauce and dill and season well with salt and pepper.

Tip the fish mixture into a gratin or pie dish. Cover the surface the sheets of filo pastry, scrunching up each sheet into a loosely crumpled ball. Brush the pastry with melted butter.

Bake in a preheated oven, 200°C (400°F), Gas Mark 6, for 20–25 minutes until the pastry is golden brown and the fish is cooked through.

For seafood & potato pie, prepare the fish mixture as above, but use 2 tablespoons chopped parsley in place of the dill. Put into a medium-sized ovenproof dish. Cook 800 g (1 lb 10 oz) chopped potatoes in a large saucepan of salted boiling water until tender. Meanwhile, put 2 large eggs in a separate saucepan and bring to the boil. Cook for 10 minutes, then plunge into cold water to cool. Shell the eggs and cut in half lengthways. Drain the potatoes and mash with 2 tablespoons butter. Season well with salt and pepper. Gently press the egg halves, at evenly spaced intervals, into the fish mixture, then spoon or pipe the mash over the fish mixture. Bake as above until the top is lightly golden and the fish is cooked through.

chillied beef parcels

Makes **6**
Preparation time **30 minutes**
Cooking time **1 hour**
10 minutes

2 teaspoons **sunflower oil**
250 g (8 oz) **minced beef**
1 small **onion**, chopped
1 **garlic clove**, finely chopped
½ teaspoon **dried crushed chillies**
¼ teaspoon **ground cinnamon**
2 teaspoons **light muscovado sugar**
1 **bay leaf**
200 g (7 oz) can **chopped tomatoes**
200 g (7 oz) can **red kidney beans**, drained
150 ml (¼ pint) **beef stock**
beaten egg, to glaze
salt and **pepper**

For the polenta pastry
300 g (10 oz) **plain flour**
50 g (2 oz) **polenta**
75 g (3 oz) **butter**, diced
75 g (3 oz) **white vegetable fat**, diced
4–4½ tablespoons **cold water**

Heat the oil in a saucepan, add the mince and onion and fry, stirring, until the mince is browned. Stir in the garlic, chillies, cinnamon, sugar and bay leaf. Mix in the tomatoes, kidney beans and stock, then add plenty of salt and pepper. Bring to the boil, stirring, then cover and simmer gently for 45 minutes. Leave to cool.

Make the pastry. Add the flour, polenta, fats and a little salt and pepper to a bowl. Rub in the fats with your fingertips or an electric mixer until you have fine crumbs. Add enough water to form a smooth dough, then knead lightly on a surface dusted with flour.

Cut the pastry in half, roll out one half and trim to a 12 × 38 cm (5 × 15 inch) rectangle, then cut into 3 × 12 cm (5 inch) squares. Spoon half the filling into the centre of the pastry squares. Brush the edges with beaten egg, then bring the points of the pastry up to the centre, pressing the straight edges of the pastry together.

Transfer to an oiled baking sheet and repeat with the remaining pastry and filling to make 6 pies. Brush the pies with beaten egg, then bake in a preheated oven, 190°C (375°F), Gas Mark 5, for 20 minutes.

Serve hot with soured cream and chunky salsa.

For herby beef pies, fry the beef and onion as above, then stir in 1 small diced carrot, 1 teaspoon dried mixed herbs, 1 teaspoon English mustard, 1 tablespoon Worcestershire sauce, 200 g (7 oz) can chopped tomatoes and 150 ml (¼ pint) beef stock. Cover and simmer for 45 minutes, then continue as above with a plain shortcrust pastry.

golden mushroom & leek pies

Serves **4**

Preparation time **15 minutes**

Cooking time **25–30 minutes**

25 g (1 oz) **butter**

2 **leeks**, thinly sliced

300 g (10 oz) **chestnut mushrooms**, quartered

300 g (10 oz) **button mushrooms**, quartered

1 tablespoon **plain flour**

250 ml (8 fl oz) **milk**

150 ml (¼ pint) **double cream**

100 g (3½ oz) **strong Cheddar cheese**, grated

4 tablespoons finely chopped **parsley**

2 sheets of **ready-rolled puff pastry**, defrosted if frozen

beaten egg, to glaze

Melt the butter in a large saucepan, add the leeks and cook for 1–2 minutes. Add the mushrooms and cook for 2 minutes. Stir in the flour and cook, stirring, for 1 minute, then gradually add the milk and cream and cook, stirring constantly, until the mixture thickens. Add the Cheddar and the parsley and cook, stirring, for 1–2 minutes. Remove from the heat.

Cut 4 rounds from the pastry sheets to cover 4 individual pie dishes. Divide the mushroom mixture between the pie dishes. Brush the rims with the beaten egg, then place the pastry rounds on top. Press down around the rims and crimp the edges with a fork. Cut a couple of slits in the top of each pie to let the steam out. Brush the pastry with the remaining egg.

Bake in a preheated oven, 220°C (425°F), Gas Mark 7, for 15–20 minutes until the pastry is golden brown. Serve immediately.

For curried ham & mushroom pies, follow the first stage above, but after cooking the mushrooms add 1 teaspoon medium curry powder and ½ teaspoon turmeric to the pan and cook, stirring, for 1 minute, before adding the flour and continuing with the recipe. Once the sauce has thickened, stir in 200 g (7 oz) cooked ham, cut into small bite-sized pieces, in place of the Cheddar and 4 tablespoons chopped coriander leaves instead of the parsley. Make and bake the pies as above.

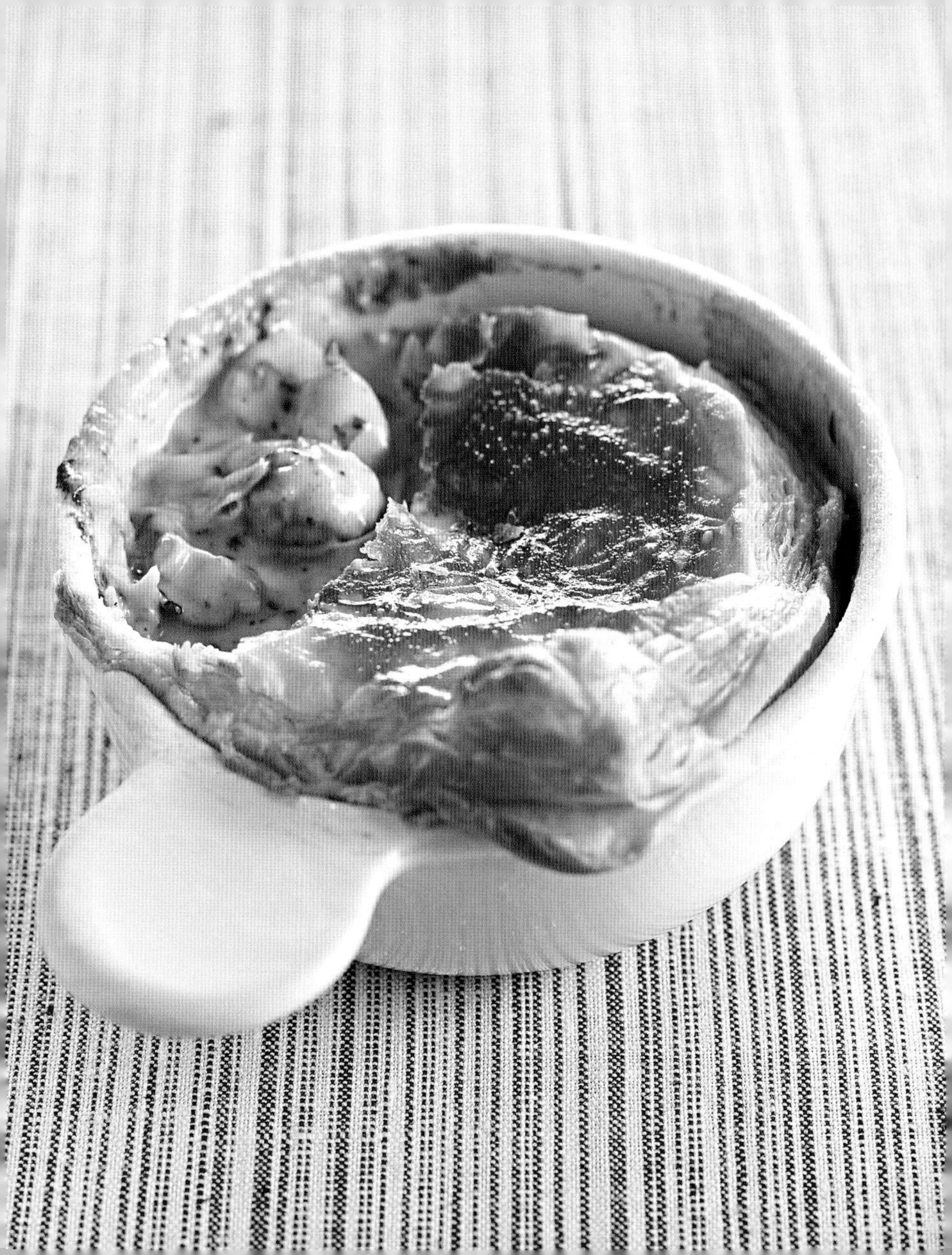

torta pasqualina

Serves **6**
Preparation time **30 minutes**,
  plus chilling
Cooking time **45–50 minutes**

1 quantity **shortcrust pastry**
  (see page 9)
175 g (6 oz) **chilled
  chargrilled artichokes
  in olive oil**
1 **onion**, chopped
2 cloves **garlic**, finely chopped
250 g (8 oz) **spinach**, rinsed,
  drained
175 g (6 oz) **cherry tomatoes**,
  halved
75 g (3 oz) **Parmesan cheese**,
  grated
4 **eggs**
250 ml (8 fl oz) **milk**
salt and **pepper**

Roll the pastry out thinly on a lightly floured surface until a little larger than a buttered 28 × 20 cm (11 × 8 inch) fluted loose-bottomed rectangular tart tin. Lift the pastry over a rolling pin, drape into the tin, then press over the base and sides. Trim off the excess pastry with scissors so that it stands a little above the top of the tin. Chill for 15 minutes.

Drain off 1 tablespoon oil from the artichokes into a frying pan, add the onion and garlic and fry for 5 minutes until softened. Scoop out of the pan and reserve. Add the spinach to the pan and fry for 2–3 minutes until just wilted. Tip into a sieve and press out the juices.

Put the tart case on a baking sheet. Arrange the spinach in the base of the pastry case, drain and arrange the artichoke hearts and halved tomatoes on top, then sprinkle with the Parmesan. Beat the eggs and milk with salt and pepper and pour into the tart.

Bake in a preheated oven, 190°C (375°F), Gas Mark 5, for 30–40 minutes until golden brown and the filling is just set. Leave to cool for 15 minutes, then remove the tart from the tin. Cut into squares and serve warm or cold.

For Italian goats' cheese tart, omit the artichokes and add 100 g (3½ oz) diced goats' cheese instead.

chicken bisteeya

Serves **6**

Preparation time **40 minutes**

Cooking time **1 hour 50 minutes**

4 **chicken thigh and drumstick joints**

1 **onion**, chopped

1 **cinnamon stick**, halved

2.5 cm (1 inch) **fresh root ginger**, finely chopped

¼ teaspoon **turmeric**

600 ml (1 pint) **water**

3 tablespoons chopped **coriander**

3 tablespoons chopped **parsley**

40 g (1½ oz) **raisins**

40 g (1½ oz) **blanched almonds**, roughly chopped

4 **eggs**

200 g (7 oz) chilled **filo pastry**

65 g (2½ oz) **butter**, melted

salt and **pepper**

To garnish

icing sugar, sifted

ground cinnamon

Pack the chicken into a large saucepan and sprinkle the onion over the top, then add the cinnamon, ginger, turmeric and salt and pepper. Cover the chicken with the measurement water. Cover and simmer for 1 hour until tender. Lift the chicken out of the stock and transfer to a plate to cool.

Boil the stock rapidly for about 10 minutes until reduced by one-third.

Dice the chicken, discarding the skin and bones. Strain the stock into a jug. Discard the cinnamon stick, then add the herbs, raisins and almonds to the chicken. Gradually whisk 200 ml (7 fl oz) of the stock into the eggs.

Brush a 23 cm (9 inch) springform tin with a little of the melted butter. Unfold the pastry, then place one of the sheets in the tin so that it half covers the base and drapes up over the side and hangs over the top of the tin. Add a second pastry sheet overlapping a little over the first and brush with a little melted butter. Continue adding pastry, brushing alternate sheets with melted butter until two-thirds of the pastry has been used and the tin is thickly covered.

Spoon in the chicken mixture, then cover with the eggs and stock. Arrange the remaining pastry over the top in a smooth layer, then fold in the sides in soft pleats, brushing layers of pastry with butter as you go. Brush the top layer with the remaining butter, then bake in a preheated oven, 180°C (350°F), Gas Mark 4, for 40–45 minutes until golden brown and the filling is set.

Leave to cool for 15 minutes, then remove from the tin. Dust with icing sugar and cinnamon and serve warm.

game pie

Serves **4**
Preparation time **45 minutes**
Cooking time **2 hours**

25 g (1 oz) **butter**
1 tablespoon **olive oil**
1 **oven-ready pheasant**,
  halved
1 **oven-ready pigeon**, halved
2 **rabbit** or **chicken leg joints**
1 large **onion**, roughly
  chopped
100 g (3½ oz) **smoked
  streaky bacon**, diced
2 tablespoons **plain flour**
200 ml (7 fl oz) **red wine**
400 ml (13 fl oz) **chicken
  stock**
2 tablespoons **redcurrant jelly**
1 teaspoon **juniper** or **allspice
  berries**, roughly crushed
1 **bouquet garni**
375 g (12 oz) **ready-made
  puff pastry**, defrosted if
  frozen
beaten egg, to glaze
salt and **pepper**

Heat the butter and oil in a large frying pan, then fry the game, in batches, until browned. Lift out and put into a large casserole dish. Add the onion and bacon to the frying pan and fry for 5 minutes, stirring until golden. Mix in the flour, then stir in the wine, stock and redcurrant jelly. Add the berries, bouquet garni and seasoning, then bring to the boil. Tip the sauce over the game, cover and cook in a preheated oven, 160°C (325°F), Gas Mark 3, for 1¼ hours. Leave to cool.

Lift out the game and take the meat off the bone. Return the meat to the sauce, discard the bouquet garni, then spoon into a 1.2 litre (2 pint) pie dish.

Roll out the pastry on a lightly floured surface until a little larger than the top of the pie dish. Cut 1 cm (½ inch) wide strips from the edges and stick on to the dish rim with beaten egg. Brush the pastry strips with egg and lay the sheet of pastry on top. Press down, trim off the excess then flute the edges. Cut leaves from the rerolled trimmings and decorate (see page 17).

Brush the pie with beaten egg, then cook in a preheated oven, 200°C (400°F), Gas Mark 6, for 30–35 minutes until golden and piping hot inside. Serve with steamed Brussels sprouts and braised red cabbage, if liked.

For beef & mushroom pie, fry 750 g (1½ lb) diced stewing beef and 150 g (5 oz) quartered mushrooms in the butter and oil. Mix with the fried onion and bacon, then the flour and stock. Continue as above but cook for 2 hours in the oven before making up the pie as above.

creamy asparagus puff pie

Serves **6**
Preparation time **25 minutes**
Cooking time **30–40 minutes**

500 g (1 lb) **ready-made puff pastry**, defrosted if frozen
1 **egg**, beaten
250 g (8 oz) bunch of **asparagus**
1 bunch of **spring onions**
1 tablespoon **olive oil**
125 g (4 oz) **mascarpone cheese**
1 large **garlic clove**, finely chopped
25 g (1 oz) **Parmesan cheese**, grated, plus extra for sprinkling
salt and **pepper**

Roll out the pastry thickly on a lightly floured surface and trim to a 23 × 30 cm (9 × 12 inch) rectangle. Transfer to an oiled baking sheet and use a little beaten egg to glaze. Mark a line 2.5 cm (1 inch) in from the edge, then prick the inside rectangle with a fork.

Bake in a preheated oven, 200°C (400°F), Gas Mark 6, for 10 minutes. Press down the centre with the back of a fork, then bake for 5–10 minutes more until the pastry is cooked through. Press down the centre once more.

Meanwhile, trim 2.5 cm (1 inch) from the base of the asparagus, then trim the spring onions to the same length. Toss the asparagus and spring onions in the oil and plenty of salt and pepper, then cook on a preheated ridged frying pan for 5 minutes, turning, until just cooked.

Beat the mascarpone with the garlic, Parmesan, remaining beaten egg and salt and pepper. Spoon into the centre of the pie case and spread into an even layer. Arrange the asparagus and spring onions alternately on top and sprinkle with a little extra Parmesan.

Bake for 10–15 minutes until the filling is just set, Check after 10 minutes and cover with kitchen foil if the pastry seems to be browning too quickly.

For asparagus & tomato puff pie, fry 1 chopped onion in 1 tablespoon oil until soft, add 2 chopped garlic cloves, 400 g (13 oz) can chopped tomatoes, 1 tablespoon sun-dried tomato paste, 1 teaspoon caster sugar, salt and pepper. Simmer for 10 minutes, stirring, until thick. Make up the pie as above, stir the Parmesan into the sauce, spread in the base of the pie, top with griddled asparagus and spring onions, then bake as above.

oriental mushroom parcels

Makes **4**
Preparation time **25 minutes**
Cooking time **25 minutes**

4 large **field mushrooms,** wiped
1 tablespoon **sesame oil**
1 tablespoon **ketjap manis** or **soy sauce**
2.5 cm (1 inch) **fresh root ginger,** peeled and finely chopped
2 **garlic cloves,** finely chopped
4 tablespoons roughly chopped **coriander**
1 **tomato,** cut into 4 thick slices
25 g (1 oz) **butter,** cut into 4 pieces
1 quantity **shortcrust pastry** (see page 9)
beaten egg, to glaze
4 teaspoons **sesame seeds,** for sprinkling
pepper

Trim the top of the mushroom stalks level with the caps, drizzle the gills with the sesame oil and ketjap manis or soy sauce, then sprinkle with the ginger, garlic and coriander. Top each with a slice of tomato, a piece of butter and a little pepper.

Cut the pastry into 4 pieces, roll out one piece thinly on a lightly floured surface to a rough-shaped 18–20 cm (7–8 inch) circle, or large enough to enclose the mushrooms (this will depend on how big they are, so make a little bigger if needed).

Place a mushroom on top of a pastry circle, brush the edges with beaten egg, then lift the pastry up and over the top of the mushroom, pleating the pastry as you go and pinching the ends together in the centre of the mushroom to completely enclose it. Repeat to make 4 parcels and put them on to a buttered baking sheet.

Brush the parcels with beaten egg and sprinkle with sesame seeds. Bake in a preheated oven, 200°C (400°F), Gas Mark 6, for about 25 minutes until golden brown. Transfer to serving plates and accompany with stir-fried vegetables and soy sauce.

For French mushroom parcels, drizzle 4 large field mushrooms with 1 tablespoon olive oil and 2 tablespoons red wine, then top with 2 finely chopped garlic cloves, 2 tablespoons chopped basil, 2 tablespoons chopped chives and 4 slices of goats' cheese cut from a 100 g (3½ oz) piece. Season the cheese with salt and pepper, then wrap in pastry, glaze with egg and top with a slice of onion. Bake as above.

goats' cheese & beetroot tart

Serves **6**
Preparation time **30 minutes**,
   plus chilling
Cooking time **45–50 minutes**

1 quantity **shortcrust pastry**
   (see page 9)
1 tablespoon **olive oil**
1 **onion**, chopped
200 g (7 oz) raw, trimmed
   beetroot, coarsely grated
4 **eggs**
250 ml (8 fl oz) **milk**
1 teaspoon **Dijon mustard**
small bunch of **thyme**
150 g (5 oz) **goats' cheese
   log**
salt and **cayenne pepper**

Roll the pastry out on a lightly floured surface until a little larger than a buttered 24 cm (9½ inch) fluted loose-bottomed tart tin. Lift the pastry over a rolling pin, drape into the tin, then press over the base and sides. Trim off the excess pastry with scissors so that it stands a little above the top of the tin. Chill for 15 minutes.

Meanwhile, heat the oil in a frying pan, add the onion and fry until softened. Add the beetroot and cook for 2–3 minutes. Beat the eggs, milk and mustard together in a bowl. Add the onions, some of the thyme leaves torn from the stems and a generous amount of salt and cayenne pepper. Leave to stand for 5 minutes.

Put the tart case on a baking sheet and pour the beetroot mix into the tart case. Cut the cheese into 6 thick slices, arrange in a ring on top of the tart and sprinkle with the remaining thyme leaves and a little salt and cayenne pepper.

Bake in a preheated oven, 180°C (350°F), Gas Mark 4, for 40–45 minutes until the filling is set. Leave to cool for 15 minutes, then remove the tin and transfer to a plate. Serve warm or cold, cut into wedges, with salad.

For minted courgette & goats' cheese tart, dice 200 g (7 oz) courgettes and add to the fried onions, fry for a few more minutes, then mix with 2 tablespoons chopped mint and 2 tablespoons chopped chives. Beat the eggs, milk, mustard and seasoning together as above, then add the courgette mix. Tip into the uncooked tart case, arrange the goats' cheese on top, season the cheese and bake as above.

venison & red wine pie

Serves **4**

Preparation time **25 minutes**

Cooking time **2 hours
50 minutes**

1 tablespoon **olive oil**

650 g (1 lb 5 oz) shoulder or
leg **venison**, diced

1 **onion**, chopped

4 **streaky bacon rashers**,
diced

2 **garlic cloves**, finely
chopped

2 tablespoons **plain flour**

300 ml (½ pint) **red wine**

450 ml (¾ pint) **beef stock**

1 tablespoon **tomato purée**

3 sprigs **rosemary**, leaves
chopped, plus extra, torn,
for sprinkling

25 g (1 oz) **butter**

300 g (10 oz) **shallots**, peeled
and halved if large

150 g (5 oz) **closed-cup
mushrooms**, thickly sliced

1 quantity **rosemary
shortcrust pastry** (see
page 10)

beaten egg, to glaze

salt and **pepper**

Heat the oil in a flameproof casserole, add the venison,
then add the onion and bacon, and fry, stirring, until the
venison is browned. Stir in the garlic and flour, then mix
in the wine, stock and tomato purée. Add the rosemary
and season well with salt and pepper.

Bring to the boil, stirring, then cover and transfer to a
preheated oven, 160°C (325°F), Gas Mark 3, for
2 hours. Take the dish out of the oven. Heat the butter
in a frying pan, add the shallots and mushrooms and fry
until golden, then stir into the venison and leave to cool.

Spoon the venison mixture into a 1.2 litre (2 pint)
ovenproof pie dish. Roll out the pastry on a lightly
floured surface until about 5 cm (2 inches) wider than
the diameter of the pie dish. Cut 2 long strips from the
edges about 1 cm (½ inch) wide. Brush the dish rim
with egg, press the strips on top, then brush these with
egg. Lift the pie lid in place, sealing the edges together
well. Trim off the excess pastry.

Flute the edge of the pastry (see page 17). Brush with
egg and sprinkle with a few extra torn rosemary leaves.
Decorate the top if liked. Bake in a preheated oven,
190°C (375°F), Gas Mark 5, for 35–40 minutes until
the pastry is golden and the filling piping hot. Serve
with green beans and braised red cabbage.

For lamb & prune pie, fry 650 g (1 lb 5 oz) sliced
lamb fillet in oil with the chopped onion and bacon as
above. Add the garlic, flour, red wine and stock, then
stir in the rosemary, 1 tablespoon redcurrant jelly and
100 g (3½ oz) pitted and halved ready-to-eat dried
prunes. Season and cook as above, then add the shallots
and mushrooms. Top with the pastry and bake as above.

mixed seafood puff pies

Makes **4**
Preparation time **30 minutes**
Cooking time **40–45 minutes**

300 g (10 oz) **white fish
fillets**, such as cod or
haddock
300 g (10 oz) **salmon fillet**,
cut into 2 pieces
600 ml (1 pint) **milk**
2 **bay leaves**
rind of 1 **lemon**, pared into
strips with a vegetable
peeler
50 g (2 oz) **butter**
50 g (2 oz) **plain flour**
150 ml (¼ pint) **fish stock**
(made with half a cube)
125 g (4 oz) **sweetcorn**
1 bunch of **spring onions**,
finely sliced
100 g (3½ oz) **Cheddar
cheese**, grated
400 g (13 oz) **frozen mixed
seafood**, defrosted, rinsed
with cold water and drained
500 g (1 lb) **ready-made puff
pastry**, defrosted if frozen
beaten egg, to glaze
salt and **pepper**

Lay the fish fillets in a frying pan, pour over just enough milk to cover, then add the bay leaves, lemon rind and salt and pepper. Cover and simmer for 8 minutes or until the fish is just cooked and flakes easily.

Lift the fish out on to a plate, peel away the skin, then break into large flakes, removing any bones. Strain the milk and mix with the remaining milk.

Heat the butter in a saucepan, stir in the flour and cook briefly, then gradually mix in the milk and bring to the boil, stirring. Stir in the fish stock and cook over a low heat for 3–4 minutes. Stir in the sweetcorn, spring onions and cheese, then season generously with salt and pepper. Cover the surface of the sauce with wetted greaseproof or nonstick paper and leave to cool.

Fold the flaked fish and mixed seafood into the sauce, then spoon into 4 individual round pie dishes. Roll the pastry out thinly on a lightly floured surface and cut out 4 pastry lids. Brush the dish rims with egg and press the lids in place. Cut fish shapes from the pastry trimmings and arrange on top, then glaze with egg.

Bake in a preheated oven, 200°C (400°F), Gas Mark 6, for 25–30 minutes until the pastry is well risen and golden and the filling is piping hot.

For smoked fish & egg puff pies, first poach 300 g (10 oz) haddock fillets and 300 g (10 oz) smoked haddock in the milk, bay leaves and lemon rind as above. Make the sauce as above, stir in the sweetcorn, spring onions and cheese, then the flaked fish, 250 g (8 oz) prawns, defrosted if frozen, and 3 hard-boiled, shelled and diced eggs. Add the pie lids and cook as above.

cockle, leek & bacon pies

Makes **6**
Preparation time **45 minutes**,
 plus chilling
Cooking time **50–55 minutes**

600 ml (1 pint) **milk**
200 g (7 oz) **leeks**, trimmed,
 thinly sliced, white and green
 parts kept separate
2 **bay leaves**
250 g (8 oz) **gammon steak**
50 g (2 oz) **butter**
50 g (2 oz) **plain flour**
200 g (7 oz) **cockles**,
 defrosted if frozen
beaten egg, to glaze
salt and **pepper**

For the pastry
375 g (12 oz) **plain flour**
175 g (6 oz) mixed **butter** and
 white vegetable fat, diced
4–4½ tablespoons **cold water**
salt and **pepper**

Pour the milk into a saucepan, add the white sliced leeks, bay leaves and salt and pepper, then bring to the boil. Set aside for 10 minutes. Grill the gammon steak on a foil-lined grill pan for 7–8 minutes, turning once, until cooked. Trim off the fat, then dice the meat.

Heat the butter in a saucepan, stir in the flour, cook for 1–2 minutes, then gradually mix in the strained milk. Bring to the boil, stirring until smooth. Discard the bay leaves, then return the white leeks to the sauce, add the green sliced leeks and cook gently for 2–3 minutes, stirring until the leeks are just cooked. Leave to cool.

Make the pastry according to the method on page 9. Wrap the dough in clingfilm and chill for 15 minutes.

Reserve one-third of the pastry, roll out the remainder thinly, then cut 6 × 15 cm (6 inch) circles. Press into buttered individual tart tins, 10 cm (4 inches) in diameter and 2.5 cm (1 inch) deep. Trim off the excess pastry and reknead and reroll the trimmings as needed.

Stir the cockles and gammon into the sauce, then spoon into the pastry bases. Brush the edges with egg. Roll out the reserved pastry and cut 12 cm (5 inch) circles for the lids. Press the pastry edges together and flute (see page 17), prick the top to let steam escape, then brush with beaten egg. Decorate (see page 17) and sprinkle with salt and pepper.

Bake the pies on a baking sheet in a preheated oven, 190°C (375°F), Gas Mark 5, for 30–35 minutes until golden brown. Serve with steamed baby carrots.

sweet pies

summer berry mille feuilles

Makes **6**
Preparation time **30 minutes**,
  plus chilling
Cooking time **15 minutes**

375 g (12 oz) **ready-made
  puff pastry**, defrosted if
  frozen
500 g (1 lb) **mixed summer
  fruits**, including sliced
  strawberries and raspberries,
  and a few blueberries
25 g (1 oz) **icing sugar**

For the vanilla custard
2 **egg yolks**
50 g (2 oz) **caster sugar**
20 g (¾ oz) **plain flour**
20 g (¾ oz) **cornflour**
150 ml (¼ pint) **double
  cream**
150 ml (¼ pint) **milk**
1 teaspoon **vanilla extract**

Roll the pastry out on a lightly floured surface and trim
to a 30 × 19 cm (12 × 7½ inch) rectangle, then cut
into 9 rectangles, each 10 × 6.5 cm (4 × 2½ inches).
Transfer to an oiled baking sheet, leaving space
between them, then chill for 15 minutes.

Bake in a preheated oven, 200°C (400°F), Gas Mark 6,
for 10–12 minutes until well risen and golden. Transfer
to a wire rack to cool.

Make the vanilla custard filling. Whisk the egg yolks
and sugar together in a large bowl, then mix in the flours.
Pour the cream and milk into a saucepan, bring to the
boil, then gradually whisk into the yolks until smooth.
Pour back into the saucepan and heat, whisking
constantly, until thick. Beat in the vanilla extract, then
take off the heat, cover the surface with a piece of
crumpled and wetted baking paper and leave to cool.

Split each pastry in half through the centre. Sandwich 3
pastry halves together with the cooked custard and fruit.
Repeat to make 6 pastry stacks. Dust with icing sugar.

Heat 3 metal skewers in a gas flame or under the grill
until very hot. Press them into the icing sugar until the
skewers form caramelized lines in the sugar. Repeat,
warming the skewers between applications when needed.

For lemon cream mille feuilles, whisk 250 ml (8 fl oz)
double cream until it forms soft swirls, then fold in
3 tablespoons lemon curd and sandwich the pastries
together with the cream instead of vanilla custard. Mix
100 g (3½ oz) sifted icing sugar with 1 tablespoon
fresh lemon juice to a smooth icing, spoon over the tops
of the pastries and decorate with lemon rind curls.

peach melba pie

Serves **6**
Preparation time **40 minutes**,
  plus cooling
Cooking time **30–35 minutes**

1 quantity **all-butter sweet
  shortcrust pastry** (see
  page 10)
75 g (3 oz) **caster sugar**,
  plus extra for sprinkling
1 teaspoon **cornflour**
grated rind of 1 **lemon**
750 g (1½ lb) **peaches**,
  halved, stoned, sliced
150 g (5 oz) **raspberries**
milk, to glaze

Reserve one-third of the pastry for the lattice. Roll out the remainder on a lightly floured surface until large enough to line the base and sides of a buttered metal pie dish, 20 cm (8 inches) in diameter and 5 cm (2 inches) deep. Lift the pastry over a rolling pin, drape into the dish, then press over the base and sides.

Mix the sugar, cornflour and lemon rind together, then add the fruits and toss together gently. Pile into the pie dish. Trim off the excess pastry, add to the reserved portion, then roll out. Cut into 1.5 cm (¾ inch) wide strips long enough to go over the top of the pie.

Brush the top edge of the pie with milk and arrange the pastry strips over the top as a lattice. Trim off the excess. Brush with milk, then sprinkle with a little sugar.

Bake in a preheated oven, 190°C (375°F), Gas Mark 5, for 30–35 minutes until golden. Leave to cool for 15 minutes, then serve cut into wedges, drizzled with melba sauce.

For melba sauce, to serve as an accompaniment, put 200 g (7 oz) raspberries in a saucepan with the juice of ½ lemon and 2 tablespoons icing sugar, and cook for 2–3 minutes until the raspberries are just tender. Cool, then purée in a blender and sieve to remove the seeds. Serve warm or cold with wedges of pie.

deep dish citrus apple pies

Makes **12**
Preparation time **40 minutes**
Cooking time **30 minutes**

750 g (1½ lb) **cooking
  apples**, quartered, cored,
  peeled and sliced
grated rind and juice of
  1 **lemon**
50 g (2 oz) **butter**
100 g (3½ oz) **caster sugar**,
  plus extra for sprinkling
juice of ½ **orange**
1 tablespoon **cornflour**
50 g (2 oz) **sultanas**
1½ quantities **all-butter
  sweet shortcrust pastry**
  (see page 10)
beaten egg or **milk**, to glaze

Toss the apple slices in the lemon rind and juice. Heat the butter in a large frying pan, add the apples, sugar and orange rind and cook gently for 5 minutes until the apples are softened but still hold their shape.

Mix the cornflour with the orange juice, add to the pan with the sultanas and cook until the juices have thickened. Take off the heat and leave to cool.

Reserve one-third of the pastry, then roll out the remainder thinly on a lightly floured surface. Stamp out 12 × 10 cm (4 inch) circles with a plain biscuit cutter and press into a buttered 12-section muffin tin.

Spoon the apple filling into the pie cases, doming it up high in the centre. Roll out the reserved pastry and any pastry trimmings, then cut out 12 × 7 cm (3 inch) lids with a fluted biscuit cutter. Brush the pie edges with milk, then press the lids on the pies. Reroll the trimmings and cut small decorations. Brush the tops of the pies with milk, add the decorations and brush these with egg or milk, then sprinkle with a little caster sugar.

Bake in a preheated oven, 190°C (375°F), Gas Mark 5, for 25 minutes until the pastry is golden. Leave to stand in the tins for 20 minutes, then loosen the edges with a knife, lift out of the tins and serve warm with custard.

For deep dish blackberry & apple pies, toss 625 g (1¼ lb) sliced cooking apples in the grated rind and juice of 1 lemon, cook gently in 50 g (2 oz) butter and sweeten with 100 g (3½ oz) caster sugar until softened. Thicken the sauce with 1 tablespoon cornflour mixed with a little water, then add 125 g (4 oz) blackberries and leave to cool. Use to fill the pies as above.

moroccan almond spiral

Serves **8**

Preparation time **30 minutes**

Cooking time **30–35 minutes**

250 g (8 oz) **butter**, at room
temperature

250 g (8 oz) **caster sugar**

3 tablespoons **runny honey**

2 **eggs**

200 g (7 oz) **ground almonds**

2 tablespoons **plain flour**

grated rind of 1 **lemon**

grated rind of 1 **orange**

100 g (3½ oz) **walnut pieces**,
finely chopped

4 teaspoons **rose water**

6 sheets of **filo pastry**,
48 × 23 cm (19 × 9 inches),
from a 270 g (8½ oz) pack,
defrosted if frozen

50 g (2 oz) melted **butter**, for
brushing

sifted **icing sugar**, for dusting

fresh or **dried rose and
lavender petals**, to decorate

Cream the butter and sugar together. Add the honey and gradually beat in the eggs. Stir in the ground almonds, flour, fruit rinds, chopped walnuts and rose water.

Unfold the pastry sheets, then arrange 5 sheets with the long edges facing you, overlapping the short edges slightly and sticking them together with a little melted butter, until you have a long continuous strip, about 2.25 metres (7 feet 5 inches) long, in all. Reserve the remaining pastry sheet in case you need to mend any broken pastry later.

Spoon or pipe the almond filling about 5 cm (2 inches) up from the bottom long edge in a long line parallel with the bottom pastry edge. Fold the sides in to enclose the filling, then fold up the base of the pastry over the filling. Now carefully roll up to the top edge of the pastry strip and stick the top edge over the roll with melted butter.

Beginning at one of the furthest ends of the almond roll, begin to coil the pastry around loosely to form a 25 cm (10 inch) diameter circle.

Tear the remaining pastry sheet into strips to mend any broken areas of pastry, sticking strips in place with melted butter. Filo pastry dries out so try to shape the pie as quickly as you can.

Lift the pastry up and slide a baking sheet underneath it. Bake in a preheated oven, 180°C (350°F), Gas Mark 4, for 30–35 minutes until golden brown. Leave to cool, then transfer to a chopping board, dust heavily with icing sugar and sprinkle with dried rose petals and lavender. Serve warm or cold, cut into wedges.

mile-high chocolate meringue pie

Serves **6**

Preparation time **40 minutes**, plus chilling

Cooking time **55–60 minutes**

For the filling

4 **eggs**, separated

175 g (6 oz) **caster sugar**

3 tablespoons **cocoa powder**, sifted

1 tablespoon **corn flour**

300 ml (½ pint) **milk**

1 teaspoon **vanilla extract**

40 g (1½ oz) **dark chocolate**, grated, plus extra to decorate

For the pastry

110 g (3¾ oz) **plain flour**

15 g (½ oz) **cocoa powder**

40 g (1½ oz) **caster sugar**

50 g (2 oz) **butter**, diced

4–5 teaspoons **cold water**

Make the pastry. Add the flour, cocoa, sugar and butter to a large bowl, then rub in with your fingertips or an electric mixer until you have fine crumbs. Mix in enough water to form a soft but not sticky dough. Roll out on a floured surface to fit a fluted loose-bottomed tart tin, 20 cm (8 inches) in diameter, 5 cm (2 inches) deep. Line the tin (see page 14). Prick the base with a fork and chill for 15 minutes. Bake the tart blind (see page 15) for 10 minutes. Remove the paper and beans and bake for a further 5 minutes.

Meanwhile, whisk the egg yolks and 50 g (2 oz) of the sugar, the cocoa powder and cornflour together in a large bowl. Pour the milk into a saucepan and bring to the boil. Gradually whisk the hot milk into the egg yolk mixture and then pour it back into the saucepan, whisking constantly until thick. Stir in the vanilla, then pour into the tart case.

Whisk the egg whites until stiff, then gradually whisk in the remaining sugar until it has all been added and the meringue is very thick, then fold in the grated chocolate. Spoon the meringue over the pie, shape into swirls, then bake at 180°C (350°F), Gas Mark 4, for 15 minutes until the meringue is golden. Cool before serving sprinkled with extra grated chocolate to decorate.

For chocolate banana cream pie, make the tart case and fill as above, then leave to cool. Cover the top with 2 sliced bananas tossed in the juice of ½ lemon. Whip 300 ml (½ pint) double cream, flavour with 2 tablespoons icing sugar and 2–3 tablespoons rum. Spoon over the top and decorate with chocolate curls.

peach & blueberry jalousie

Serves **6**
Preparation time **30 minutes**
Cooking time **20–25 minutes**

500 g (1 lb) chilled **ready-made puff pastry**
4 **ripe peaches** or **nectarines**, halved, stoned and thickly sliced
125 g (4 oz) **blueberries**
50 g (2 oz) **caster sugar**, plus a little extra for sprinkling
grated rind of ½ **lemon**
1 **egg**, beaten
icing sugar, for dusting
beaten egg, to glaze

Roll out half the pastry on a lightly floured surface and trim to a 30 x 18 cm (12 x 7 inch) rectangle. Transfer to a lightly oiled baking sheet.

Pile the peach or nectarine slices on top, leaving a 2.5 cm (1 inch) border of pastry showing, then sprinkle on the blueberries, sugar and lemon rind. Brush the pastry border with a little beaten egg.

Roll out the remaining pastry to a little larger than the first piece, then trim to 33 x 20 cm (13 x 8 inches). Fold in half lengthways, then make cuts in from the fold about 1 cm (½ inch) apart and about 6 cm (2½ inches) long, leaving a wide uncut border of pastry.

Lift the pastry over the fruit, unfold so that the fruit and bottom layer of pastry are completely covered, then press the pastry edges together. Trim if needed. Knock up the edges with a knife, then flute (see page 17).

Brush the top of the pastry with beaten egg, sprinkle with a little extra sugar and bake in a preheated oven, 200°C (400°F), Gas Mark 6, for 20–25 minutes until the pastry is well risen and golden brown. Dust with icing sugar and serve cut into squares, warm or cold, with cream or ice cream.

For apple & blackberry jalousie, replace the peaches and blueberries with 4 Granny Smith apples, quartered, cored and thickly sliced, and 125 g (4 oz) blackberries.

gooseberry & elderflower pies

Makes **4**
Preparation time **30 minutes**
Cooking time **20–25 minutes**

125 g (4 oz) **caster sugar**,
plus extra for sprinkling
2 teaspoons **cornflour**
400 g (13 oz) **gooseberries**,
topped and tailed
1 quantity **lemon-flavoured
pâte sucrée**, chilled (see
page 11)
1 tablespoon **elderflower
cordial**, undiluted
milk or **beaten egg**, to glaze

Mix the sugar, cornflour and gooseberries together in a
bowl. Cut the pastry into 4 pieces, then roll each piece
out to a rough-shaped 18 cm (7 inch) circle. Drape
each piece into a buttered individual Yorkshire pudding
tin, 10 cm (4 inches) in diameter and 2.5 cm (1 inch)
deep, leaving the excess pastry overhanging the edges
of the tins.

Spoon in the gooseberry mixture and mound up in the
centre, then drizzle over the elderflower cordial. Fold the
overhanging pastry up and over the filling, pleating
where needed and leaving the centres of the pies open.

Brush the pastry with milk or beaten egg, sprinkle with
a little sugar and bake in a preheated oven, 190°C
(375°F), Gas Mark 5, for 20–25 minutes until golden.
Leave to stand for 15 minutes, then loosen the edges
and lift the pies out of the tins. Serve with elderflower
cream (see below).

For elderflower cream, to serve as an accompaniment,
whip 200 ml (7 fl oz) double cream, then fold in
2 tablespoons undiluted elderflower cordial and the
grated rind of ½ lemon.

deep dish puff apple pie

Serves **6**
Preparation time **40 minutes**
Cooking time **20–25 minutes**

1 kg (2 lb) or about 5 **cooking apples**, quartered, cored, peeled and thickly sliced
100 g (3½ oz) **caster sugar**, plus extra for sprinkling
grated rind of 1 small **orange**
½ teaspoon **ground mixed spice** or **ground cinnamon**
3 whole **cloves**
400 g (13 oz) chilled **ready-made puff pastry**
beaten egg, to glaze

Fill a 1.2 litre (2 pint) pie dish with the apples. Mix the sugar with the orange rind, mixed spice or cinnamon and cloves, then sprinkle over the apples.

Roll the pastry out on a lightly floured surface until a little larger than the top of the dish. Cut 2 long strips from the edges, about 1 cm (½ inch) wide. Brush the dish rim with a little beaten egg, press the strips on top, then brush these with egg (see page 16). Lift the remaining pastry over the dish and press the edges together well.

Trim off the excess pastry, knock up the edges with a small knife, then flute (see pages 17). Reroll the trimmings and cut out small heart shapes or circles with a small biscuit cutter. Brush the top of the pie with beaten egg, add the pastry shapes, then brush these with egg. Sprinkle with a little extra sugar.

Bake in a preheated oven, 200°C (400°F), Gas Mark 6, for 20–25 minutes until the pastry is well risen and golden. Serve warm with spoonfuls of crème fraîche or extra-thick cream.

For spiced plum & pear pie, substitute 500 g (1 lb) sliced pears and 500 g (1 lb) sliced plums for the apples, sprinkle with 75 g (3 oz) caster sugar and add 2 halved star anise, 3 cloves and ¼ teaspoon ground cinnamon. Omit the fruit rind, then cover with the pastry and continue as above.

mixed berry pies

Makes **12**
Preparation time **40 minutes**
Cooking time **30–35 minutes**

400 g (13 oz) mixed
  **redcurrants and
  blackcurrants** or all
  blackcurrants
2 tablespoons **water**
150 g (5 oz) **caster sugar**,
  plus extra for sprinkling
1 tablespoon **cornflour**
175 g (6 oz) **raspberries**
200 g (7 oz) small
  strawberries, quartered
1½ quantities **all-butter
  sweet shortcrust pastry**
  (see page 10)
milk, to glaze

Cook the currants with the measurement water and sugar in a saucepan for 5 minutes, stirring until soft. Mix the cornflour with a little extra water until a smooth paste, then stir into the fruit and cook until thickened. Add the raspberries and strawberries, stir gently together, then leave to cool.

Reserve one-third of the pastry, then roll out the remainder thinly on a lightly floured surface. Stamp out 12 × 10 cm (4 inch) circles with a fluted biscuit cutter and press into a buttered 12-section muffin tin. Reknead and reroll the pastry trimmings as needed.

Spoon the fruit into the pies. Roll out the reserved pastry and any pastry trimmings and cut out 12 × 7 cm (3 inch) lids with a fluted biscuit cutter. Cut a small flower, heart or star in the centre of each. Brush the top edges of the fruit-filled pies with a little milk, add the pastry lids and press the edges together well to seal.

Brush the pies with a little milk and sprinkle with sugar. Bake in a preheated oven, 180°C (350°F), Gas Mark 4, for 25–30 minutes until golden. Leave to stand in the tins for 20 minutes, then loosen the edges with a knife and lift out of the tins. Serve warm with cream.

For plum & strawberry pies, cook 500 g (1 lb) stoned and diced plums with the water and sugar as above. Thicken with the cornflour mixed with water, then add 250 g (8 oz) quartered strawberries. Use to fill the pies as above.

lemon meringue pie

Serves **6**

Preparation time **40 minutes**,
  plus chilling

Cooking time **35–40 minutes**

375 g (12 oz) chilled ready-
  made or homemade **sweet
  shortcrust pastry** (see
  page 10)
200 g (7 oz) **caster sugar**
40 g (1½ oz) **cornflour**
grated rind and juice of
  2 lemons
4 **eggs**, separated
200–250 ml (7–8 fl oz) **water**

Roll out the pastry thinly on a lightly floured surface
and use to line a 20 cm (8 inch) diameter x 5 cm
(2 inch) deep fluted loose-bottomed flan tin, pressing
evenly into the sides (see page 14). Trim the top and
prick the base. Chill for 15 minutes. Line the tart with
nonstick baking paper, add baking beans and bake in
a preheated oven, 190°C (375°F), Gas Mark 5, for
15 minutes. Remove the paper and beans and bake
for a further 5 minutes.

Put 75 g (3 oz) of the sugar in a bowl with the
cornflour and lemon rind, add the egg yolks and mix
until smooth. Make the lemon juice up to 300 ml
(½ pint) with the measurement water, pour into a
saucepan and bring to the boil. Gradually mix into the
yolk mixture, whisking until smooth. Pour back into
the pan and bring to the boil, whisking until very thick.
Pour into the pastry case and spread level.

Whisk the egg whites until they form stiff peaks.
Gradually whisk in the remaining sugar, a teaspoonful
at a time, then whisk for 1–2 minutes more until thick
and glossy. Spoon over the lemon layer to cover
completely and swirl with a spoon.

Reduce the oven temperature to 180°C (350°F),
Gas Mark 4, and cook for 15–20 minutes until the
meringue is golden and cooked through. Leave to stand
for 15 minutes, then remove the tart tin and transfer to
a serving plate. Serve warm or cold with cream.

For citrus meringue pie, mix the grated rind of 1 lime,
1 lemon and ½ small orange with the cornflour.
Squeeze the juice from the fruits and make up to
300 ml (½ pint) with water. Continue as above.

apricot & pistachio purses

Makes **8**

Preparation time **25 minutes**,
plus chilling

Cooking time **15 minutes**

75 g (3 oz) **butter**, at room
temperature

25 g (1 oz) **caster sugar**

few drops of **almond essence**
or **orange flower water**

1 small **egg yolk**

25 g (1 oz) **ground almonds**

25 g (1 oz) **pistachio nuts**,
roughly chopped

8 **apricots**

4 sheets of **filo pastry**,
48 × 23 cm (19 × 9 inches),
from a 270 g (8¾ oz) pack,
defrosted if frozen

sifted **icing sugar**, for dusting

Cream 25 g (1 oz) of the butter with the sugar and
almond essence or orange flower water until light and
pale. Add the egg yolk and ground almonds, mix until
smooth, then stir in the pistachios. Chill for 15 minutes.

Cut each apricot in half, remove the stones, then
sandwich the apricots back together with the pistachio
mixture in the middle.

Melt the remaining butter. Unfold the pastry sheets and
put one sheet on your work surface. Brush with melted
butter, then cut into 4 rectangles. Put an apricot on one
of the rectangles, lift up the corners of the pastry to
enclose the apricot, then pinch together at the top of
the fruit. Wrap with a second pastry rectangle at right
angles to the first to form a purse shape. Repeat with
a second apricot and 2 more pastry rectangles, then
place on a baking sheet. Continue until all apricots have
been used.

Brush with a little of the remaining butter, then bake in
a preheated oven, 190°C (375°F), Gas Mark 5, for 15
minutes until golden. Dust with icing sugar and serve
warm or cold with scoops of vanilla ice cream.

For apple strudel purses, omit the almond essence
or orange flower water and pistachios from the
creamed mixture, adding an extra 25 g (1 oz) ground
almonds and ¼ teaspoon ground cinnamon, then stir
in 2 cored, peeled and diced dessert apples and
40 g (1½ oz) sultanas. Divide the mixture between
8 rectangles of pastry, wrap the pastry around the
filling, then enclose each in a second pastry rectangle
and continue as above.

sweet cherry pies

Makes **4**
Preparation time **30 minutes**
Cooking time **20–25 minutes**

125 g (4 oz) **caster sugar**,
plus extra for sprinkling
1 tablespoon **cornflour**
½ teaspoon **ground star
anise** or **cinnamon**
500 g (1 lb) **frozen pitted
black cherries**, just
defrosted, halved
1 quantity **all-butter sweet
shortcrust pastry** (see page
10), flavoured with grated
orange rind, chilled
milk or **beaten egg**, to glaze

Mix the sugar, cornflour and star anise together, then add the cherries and toss together.

Roll out two-thirds of the pastry thinly on a lightly floured surface. Use to line 4 fluted loose-bottomed 10 cm (4 inch) tart tins, rerolling the pastry trimmings as needed.

Spoon the cherry mixture into the pastry cases, and brush the top edges with milk or beaten egg. Roll out the reserved pastry with any trimmings and and cut 4 x 10 cm (4 inch) circles with a fluted biscuit cutter.

Add the pie lids and press the pastry edges together to seal. Slash the tops with a knife, then brush the tops with milk or beaten egg and sprinkle with a little extra sugar.

Bake in a preheated oven, 180°C (350°F), Gas Mark 4, for 20–25 minutes until the pastry is golden. Leave to stand for 15 minutes, then loosen the edges of the pies and take out of the tin. Serve warm or cold with custard.

For kirsch custard, to serve as an accompaniment, whisk 3 egg yolks with 3 tablespoons caster sugar and 2 teaspoons cornflour until smooth. Heat 300 ml (½ pint) milk just to boiling point, gradually whisk into the yolks, pour back into the pan and heat gently, slowly bringing almost to the boil until thickened. Take off the heat and stir in 2 tablespoons kirsch liqueur.

sweet potato meringue pie

Serves **6**
Preparation time **30 minutes**,
  plus chilling
Cooking time **1 hour**
  5 minutes

1 quantity **sweet shortcrust
  pastry** (see page 10)
500 g (1 lb) **sweet potato**,
  peeled and diced
150 ml (¼ pint) **double
  cream**
75 g (3 oz) **light muscovado
  sugar**
2 tablespoons **runny honey**
1 teaspoon **ground ginger**
1 teaspoon **mixed spice**
1 **egg**
3 **egg yolks**

For the meringue topping
3 **egg whites**
50 g (2 oz) **light muscovado
  sugar**
50 g (2 oz) **caster sugar**
½ teaspoon **ground ginger**

Roll the pastry out on a lightly floured surface until large enough to line a buttered metal pie dish, 20 cm (8 inches) in diameter and 5 cm (2 inches) deep. Lift the pastry over a rolling pin, drape into the tin then press over the base and sides. Trim the edges, then chill for 15 minutes.

Put the sweet potato in the top of a steamer, cover and cook for 10 minutes or until tender. Mash with the cream, sugar, honey and spices, then beat in the whole egg and egg yolks. Pour into the pie case, level the surface, then bake in a preheated oven, 180°C (350°F), Gas Mark 4, for 40 minutes until set.

Make the topping. Whisk the egg whites until you have stiff peaks, then gradually whisk in the sugars, a teaspoonful at a time, until all the sugar has been added. Add the ginger and whisk for a minute or two more until very thick and glossy. Spoon over the hot pie and swirl the meringue with the back of a spoon. Bake for 15 minutes until lightly browned and the meringue is crisp.

Leave to cool for 30 minutes, then cut into wedges and serve warm with scoops of vanilla ice cream.

For spiced pumpkin meringue pie, omit the sweet potato and add 500 g (1 lb) deseeded pumpkin instead. Peel, dice and steam as above, mash with the cream, spices and egg yolks and bake in the pie case. Top with the meringue and return to the oven as above.

gâteau pithiviers with plums

Serves **6**
Preparation time **30 minutes**
Cooking time **25–30 minutes**

100 g (3½ oz) **unsalted
    butter**, at room temperature
100 g (3½ oz) **caster sugar**
100 g (3½ oz) **ground
    almonds**
few drops of **almond essence**
1 **egg**, beaten, plus extra to
    glaze
500 g (1 lb) chilled **ready-
    made puff pastry**
375 g (12 oz) **plums**, pitted
    and thickly sliced
sifted **icing sugar**, for dusting

Cream the butter and sugar together in a bowl until pale and smooth. Add the almonds and almond essence, then the egg, and mix together until smooth.

Roll out half the pastry thinly on a lightly floured surface and trim to a 25 cm (10 inch) circle using a dinner plate as a guide. Place on a wetted baking sheet, then spread the almond paste over the top, leaving a 2.5 cm (1 inch) border of pastry around the edges. Arrange the plums in a single layer on top. Brush the pastry border with a little beaten egg.

Roll out the remaining pastry thinly and trim to a circle a little larger than the first. Cut 5 or 6 swirly 'S' shapes out of the centre of the pastry, then lift over a rolling pin and position on the almond paste. Press the edges together to seal and trim to neaten if needed. Knock up the edge to separate the pastry layers slightly, then flute (see page 17).

Brush the top with beaten egg and bake in a preheated oven, 200°C (400°F), Gas Mark 6, for 25–30 minutes until well risen and golden.

Leave to cool slightly, then dust the top with icing sugar and serve cut into wedges with cream.

For brandied prune Pithiviers, soak 150 g (5 oz) ready-to-eat pitted prunes in 3 tablespoons brandy, then arrange over the almond paste instead of the plums. Continue as above.

autumn fruit pies

Makes **6**

Preparation time **35 minutes**, plus cooling

Cooking time **45–50 minutes**

175 g (6 oz) **blackcurrants**

125 g (4 oz) **caster sugar**, plus extra for sprinkling

2 tablespoons **water**

1 tablespoon **cornflour**

1 teaspoon **ground cinnamon**, plus extra for sprinkling

grated rind of 1 **orange**

375 g (12 oz) **ripe plums**, stoned and diced

150 g (5 oz) **blackberries**

milk, to glaze

For the hot water crust pastry

175 g (6 oz) **lard**

175 ml (6 fl oz) **milk** and **water**, mixed half and half

50 g (2 oz) **caster sugar**

375 g (12 oz) **plain flour**

¼ teaspoon **salt**

Make the hot water crust pastry (see page 11), adding the sugar when heating the lard and milk-and-water mix. Leave to cool for 20 minutes while making the filling.

Put the blackcurrants, sugar and water in a saucepan and heat for 5 minutes until soft. Mix the cornflour to a paste with a little extra water, add to the pan and cook, stirring until thickened. Take off the heat and stir in the cinnamon, orange rind, plums and blackberries. Set aside.

Reserve one-third of the warm pastry, then cut the remainder into 6 pieces. Press one piece over the base, up and slightly above the top of a 250 ml (8 fl oz) individual pudding mould. Repeat with 5 more moulds.

Spoon in the filling. Cut the reserved pastry into 6, then roll out each on a lightly floured surface to form lids. Cut small heart shapes in the centre of each lid. Place over the filling and press the edges together well. Trim off the excess pastry and flute the edges (see page 17). Brush with milk and sprinkle with extra sugar and cinnamon.

Put the moulds on a baking sheet, then bake in a preheated oven, 180°C (350°F), Gas Mark 4, for 40–45 minutes until golden. Cover with foil after 30 minutes. Leave to cool for 10 minutes, then serve in the moulds.

For redcurrant & pear pies, make up the pastry as above. Omit the blackcurrants and cook 175 g (6 oz) redcurrants with the sugar and water until softened. Thicken with the cornflour, take off the heat, then stir in the orange rind, 375 g (12 oz) cored, peeled and diced pears and 150 g (5 oz) raspberries in place of the plums and blackberries. Finish as above.

pumpkin pie

Serves **6**
Preparation time **30 minutes**
Cooking time **1–1¼ hours**,
  plus cooling

500 g (1 lb) **pumpkin** or
  butternut squash, weighed
  after deseeding and peeling
3 **eggs**
100 g (3½ oz) **light
  muscovado sugar**
2 tablespoons **plain flour**
½ teaspoon **ground
  cinnamon**
½ teaspoon **ground ginger**
¼ teaspoon **grated nutmeg**
200 ml (7 fl oz) **milk**, plus
  extra to glaze
450 g (14½ oz) chilled ready-
  made or homemade **sweet
  shortcrust pastry** (see
  page 10)
sifted **icing sugar**, for dusting

Cut the pumpkin or butternut squash into cubes and cook in a covered steamer for 15–20 minutes or until tender. Cool, then purée in a liquidizer or food processor.

Whisk the eggs, sugar, flour and spices together in a bowl until just mixed. Add the pumpkin purée, whisk together, then gradually mix in the milk. Set aside.

Roll out three-quarters of the pastry on a lightly floured surface until large enough to line a buttered 23 cm (9 inch) x 2.5 cm (1 inch) deep enamel pie dish. Lift the pastry over a rolling pin, drape into the dish and press over the base and sides. Trim off the excess and add the trimmings to the reserved pastry. Roll out thinly and cut tiny leaves, then mark veins (see page 17). Brush the pastry rim with milk, then press on the leaves around the rim, reserving a few. Put the pie on a baking sheet.

Pour the pumpkin filling into the dish, add a few leaf decorations on top of the filling if liked, then brush these and the dish edges lightly with milk. Bake in a preheated oven, 190°C (375°F), Gas Mark 5, for 45–55 minutes until the filling is set and the pastry cooked through. Cover with foil after 20 minutes to stop the pastry edge from overbrowning.

Serve dusted with a little icing sugar, with whipped cream sprinkled with a little extra ground spice, if liked.

For gingered pumpkin pie with maple syrup, omit the muscovado sugar and add 6 tablespoons maple syrup. Omit the ground cinnamon and nutmeg and increase the ground ginger to 1½ teaspoons, adding 2 tablespoons finely chopped glacé or stem ginger.

sweet cranberry & orange pie

Serves **6–8**
Preparation time **30 minutes**,
  plus cooling
Cooking time **35–40 minutes**

500 g (1 lb) **frozen
  cranberries**
150 g (5 oz) **caster sugar**
grated rind and juice of
  1 orange
2 tablespoons **water**
1 tablespoon **cornflour**
500 g (1 lb) **ready-made puff
  pastry**, defrosted if frozen
beaten egg, to glaze

To decorate
100 g (3½ oz) **icing sugar**,
  sifted
grated rind and juice of ½
  orange

Cook the cranberries in a saucepan with the sugar, orange rind and juice and the measurement water for 10 minutes, stirring occasionally until the cranberries are soft. Mix the cornflour to a paste with a little extra water, add to the cranberries and cook for a few minutes, stirring until thickened, then leave to cool.

Cut the pastry in half, roll out one half on a lightly floured surface and trim to a 20 × 25 cm (8 × 10 inch) rectangle, then transfer to a buttered baking sheet. Brush the egg in a border around the edge of the rectangle, then pile the cranberry mixture in the middle.

Roll out the remaining pastry a little larger than the first and drape over the cranberries. Press the pastry edges together to seal well, then trim the top pastry layer to match the lower one. Knock up the edges of the pastry, then flute (see page 17).

Brush the top with egg, then bake in a preheated oven, 200°F (400°F), Gas Mark 6, for 25–30 minutes until well risen and golden brown. Leave to cool for 30 minutes.

Mix the icing sugar with enough of the orange juice to make a smooth icing that just falls from a spoon, then drizzle randomly over the pie to decorate and sprinkle with the grated orange rind. Set aside for 20 minutes or until the icing is set, then cut into strips to serve.

For mixed berry pie, cook a 500 g (1 lb) bag of mixed frozen blackberries, cherries and currants with 100 g (3½ oz) caster sugar and the rind and juice of 1 orange, but no extra water. Thicken with cornflour and finish as above, dusting the top with icing sugar instead of the icing.

154

chocolate cream pie

Serves **6–8**
Preparation time **30 minutes**,
 plus chilling and cooling
Cooking time **45–50 minutes**

1 quantity **chocolate all-
 butter sweet shortcrust
 pastry**, chilled (see page
 10), made by replacing
 15 g (½ oz) flour with cocoa
 powder
150 g (5 oz) **plain dark
 chocolate**, broken into
 pieces
500 g (1lb) **medium-fat soft
 cheese**, softened
100 g (3½ oz) **caster sugar**
1 tablespoon **plain flour**
1 teaspoon **vanilla extract**
3 **eggs**

Roll the pastry out on a lightly floured surface a little
larger than a buttered 23 cm (9 inch) fluted loose-
bottomed tart tin 3.5 cm (1½ inches) deep. Press the
pastry over the base and sides and trim off the excess
with scissors so it stands just above the top of the tin.
Prick the base with a fork, then chill for 15 minutes.

Bake the tart blind (see page 15) for 15 minutes.
Remove the paper and baking beans and cook for a
further 5 minutes. Reduce the oven temperature to
150°C (300°F), Gas Mark 2.

Meanwhile, melt the chocolate in a bowl over hot water.
Put the cream cheese in a bowl, add the sugar, flour
and vanilla extract, then gradually beat in the eggs until
smooth. Ladle about one-third into the chocolate bowl
and mix until smooth.

Pour the vanilla cheese mixture into the tart case, then
pipe over the chocolate mixture over the top and swirl
together with the handle of a teaspoon for a marbled
effect. Bake for 30–35 minutes until set around the
edges, beginning to crack and the centre still wobbles
slightly. Leave to cool in the turned-off oven.

When cool, refrigerate overnight. Remove the pie from
the tin, put it on a plate and serve cut into wedges.

For vanilla cream pie, make a plain tart case with
all-butter sweet shortcrust pastry, omitting the cocoa
powder. Bake blind, then fill with the vanilla cheese
mixture omitting the melted chocolate and adding
50 g (2 oz) sultanas and the grated rind of 1 lemon
instead. Bake as above, then top with 200 ml (7 fl oz)
whipped double cream before serving.

blackberry & apple streusel pie

Serves **8–10**
Preparation time **40 minutes**,
    plus chilling
Cooking time **40–45 minutes**

375 g (12 oz) **plain flour**
125 g (4 oz) **caster sugar**
175 g (6 oz) **butter**, diced
50 g (2 oz) **flaked almonds**
3–3½ tablespoons **cold water**
sifted **icing sugar**, for dusting

For the filling
75 g (3 oz) **caster sugar**
2 teaspoons **cornflour**
1 kg (2 lb) **cooking apples**
200 g (7 oz) **blackberries**

Add the flour, sugar and butter to a large bowl and rub in with your fingertips or an electric mixer until you have fine crumbs. Measure out 250 g (8 oz), add the flaked almonds and reserve this for the streusel topping.

Mix in just enough water to the remaining pastry crumbs to form a soft but not sticky dough. Knead lightly until smooth, then roll out on a floured surface until a little larger than a buttered 28 cm (11 inch) fluted loose-bottomed tart tin. Lift the pastry over a rolling pin, drape into the tin, then press over the base and sides. Trim off the excess pastry with scissors so that it stands a little above the top of the tin. Chill for 15 minutes.

Make the filling. Mix the sugar and cornflour together. Quarter, core and peel the apples, slice and add to the sugar mix with the blackberries. Toss together gently, then pile into the tart tin. Spoon the streusel mix on top and stand the tin on a baking sheet.

Bake in a preheated oven, 190°C (375°F), Gas Mark 5, for 40–45 minutes, checking after 25 minutes and covering with foil if the almonds and edge of the pastry seem to be browning too quickly. Leave to cool in the tin for 15 minutes, then dust the top with icing sugar. Remove the pie from the tin and cut into wedges. Serve with spoonfuls of clotted cream.

For Christmas apple & mincemeat pie, make up the tart case and streusel topping as above. Fill with 1 kg (2 lb) peeled, cored and sliced apples, 200 g (7 oz) Christmas mincemeat and 2 tablespoons chopped glacé ginger. Sprinkle with the streusel topping and bake as above.

sweet tarts

minted fig tarts

Makes **12**
Preparation time **30 minutes**,
    plus chilling and cooling
Cooking time **9–10 minutes**

1 quantity **pâte sucrée** (see
    page 11), chilled
300 ml (½ pint) **double
    cream**
200 g (7 oz) **Greek yogurt**
2 tablespoons **thick-set
    Greek honey**, plus extra for
    drizzling
4 tablespoons chopped **mint**
12 **figs**
tiny **mint leaves**, to decorate

Roll the pastry out thinly on a lightly floured surface, then stamp out 12 × 10 cm (4 inch) circles with a fluted biscuit cutter and press into a buttered 12-section muffin tin. Reknead and reroll the pastry trimmings as needed. Prick the bases of each tart 2–3 times with a fork, then chill for 15 minutes.

Line the tarts with squares of nonstick baking paper and baking beans and bake in a preheated oven, 190°C (375°F), Gas Mark 5, for 5 minutes. Remove the paper and beans and cook for a further 4–5 minutes until golden. Leave to cool for 10 minutes, then loosen the edges and transfer to a wire rack to cool.

Whip the cream to form soft swirls, then fold in the yogurt, honey and mint. Spoon into the tart cases. Cut the figs into wedges and arrange over the top of the tarts. Drizzle with extra honey and sprinkle with tiny mint leaves just before serving.

For minted plum tarts, make and fill the tarts as above, then slice 9 ripe plums and lightly fry in 25 g (1 oz) butter with 1 tablespoon honey until hot. Spoon over the tarts and serve immediately.

strawberry chiffon tart

Serves **6**
Preparation time **40 minutes**,
 plus chilling and cooling
Cooking time **20 minutes**

1 quantity **pâte sucrée** (see
 page 11), chilled
6 small **strawberries** with
 hulls, to decorate

For the filling
2 tablespoons **water**
1½ teaspoons **powdered
 gelatine**
150 g (5 oz) **strawberries**,
 hulled and sliced
150 ml (¼ pint) **double
 cream**
150 g (5 oz) **Greek yogurt**
2 tablespoons **icing sugar**
few drops of **vanilla extract**

For the jelly topping
1½ teaspoons **powdered
 gelatine**
6 tablespoons **water**
250 g (8 oz) **strawberries**,
 hulled
2 tablespoons **icing sugar**
few drops of **vanilla extract**

Roll out the pastry on a floured surface until a little larger than a buttered loose-bottomed fluted tart tin with sloping sides, 20 cm (8 inches) in diameter at the top and 5 cm (2 inches) deep. Press the pastry over the base and sides and trim off the excess so it stands a little above the top of the tin. Prick the base with a fork, then chill for 15 minutes. Bake blind (see page 15) and leave to cool.

Make the filling. Add the water to a small heatproof bowl, then sprinkle over the gelatine, making sure it is completely absorbed by the water. Leave for 5 minutes. Stand the bowl in a pan of gently simmering water and leave until the gelatine has completely dissolved to a clear liquid.

Purée the strawberries, then sieve. Whip the cream to form soft swirls, then fold in the yogurt, strawberry purée, sugar and vanilla. Gradually add the dissolved gelatine, pour into the tart case and chill for 1 hour.

Make the jelly topping. Sprinkle the gelatine over 2 tablespoons water and leave to soak as before. Add the strawberries to a saucepan with the remaining water and sugar, and cook for 5 minutes, mashing until soft. Take off the heat and stir in the gelatine until dissolved. Purée until smooth, then add the vanilla. Leave to cool.

Pour the jelly over the top of the tart, add the small strawberries around the edge of the tart and chill for 2–3 hours or until set. Remove the tart from the tin, transfer to a serving plate and cut into portions.

For blackberry & cassis chiffon tart, make up the tart case and filling as above, using blackberries instead of the strawberries and omitting the vanilla. Add 2 tablespoons cassis liqueur to the jelly layer.

french apple flan

Makes **4**

Preparation time **20 minutes**, plus chilling

Cooking time **25–30 minutes**

375 g (12 oz) **ready-made puff pastry**

2 **crisp green dessert apples** (such as Granny Smith), peeled, cored and sliced

1 tablespoon **caster sugar**

25 g (1 oz) **unsalted butter**, chilled

crème fraîche, to serve

For the apricot glaze

250 g (8 oz) **apricot jam**

2 teaspoons **lemon juice**

2 teaspoons **water**

Cut the pastry into 4, then roll out each piece on a lightly floured surface until 2 mm (⅛ inch) thick. Cut out 4 circles using a 13 cm (5½ inch) plate as a guide, – make a number of short cuts around the plate rather than drawing the knife around, which can stretch the pastry. Place on a baking sheet.

Place a slightly smaller plate on each pastry circle and score around the edge to form a 1 cm (½ inch) border. Prick the centres with a fork and chill for 30 minutes.

Arrange the apple slices in a circle over the pastry rounds and sprinkle with the sugar. Grate the butter over the top and bake in a preheated oven, 220°C (425°F), Gas Mark 7, for 25–30 minutes until the pastry and apples are golden.

Meanwhile, make the apricot glaze. Put the jam in a small saucepan with the lemon juice and the measurement water and heat gently until the jam melts. Increase the heat and boil for 1 minute, remove from the heat and press through a fine sieve. Keep warm, then brush over each apple tart while they are still warm. Serve with ice cream.

For peach tartlets, replace the 2 apples with 2 peaches, halved, skinned and thinly sliced. Arrange on the pastry circles and continue as above, baking for 12–15 minutes.

classic lemon tart

Serves **8**
Preparation time **20 minutes**,
  plus chilling
Cooking time **40–45 minutes**

3 **eggs**
1 **egg yolk**
475 ml (16 fl oz) **double cream**
100 g (3½ oz) **sugar**
150 ml (¼ pint) **lemon juice**

For the pastry
200 g (7 oz) **plain flour**
½ teaspoon **salt**
100 g (3½ oz) **butter**, diced
2 tablespoons **icing sugar**,
  plus extra for dusting
2 **egg yolks**
1–2 teaspoons **cold water**

Make the pastry. Put the flour and salt in a mixing bowl, add the butter and rub in with your fingertips or using an electric mixer until you have fine crumbs.

Stir in the icing sugar and gradually work in the egg yolks and the measurement water to form a firm dough.

Knead the dough briefly on a lightly floured surface, then wrap with clingfilm and chill for 30 minutes. Roll out the dough and use to line a 25 cm (10 inch) fluted pie dish or tart tin. Prick the pastry case with a fork and chill for 20 minutes.

Line the pastry case with nonstick baking paper and baking beans and bake in a preheated oven, 200°C (400°F), Gas Mark 6, for 10 minutes. Remove the paper and beans and bake for a further 10 minutes until crisp and golden. Remove from the oven and reduce the oven temperature to 150°C (300°F), Gas Mark 2.

Beat together all the filling ingredients, pour them into the pastry case and bake for 20–25 minutes, or until the filling is just set. Let the tart cool completely, dust with sifted icing sugar and serve.

For dark chocolate tart, make the tart base as above and bake blind. Heat 450 ml (¾ pint) double cream in a saucepan with 150 g (5 oz) plain dark chocolate, stirring until the chocolate has melted. Whisk 3 eggs and 1 egg yolk with 50 g (2 oz) caster sugar and ¼ teaspoon ground cinnamon. Gradually whisk in the chocolate cream. Bake as above and serve cold, dusted with sifted cocoa powder.

double chocolate & hazelnut tarts

Makes **6**
Preparation time **30 minutes**,
   plus chilling and cooling
Cooking time **12 minutes**

1 quantity **pâte sucrée with
   hazelnuts** (see page 11),
   chilled
200 g (7 oz) **plain dark
   chocolate**, broken into
   pieces
15 g (½ oz) **butter**
3 **eggs**, separated
350 ml (12 fl oz) **double
   cream**
2 tablespoons **icing sugar**
100 g (3½ oz) **white
   chocolate**, broken into
   pieces
4 teaspoons **kahlua** or **Irish
   cream liqueur**
50 g (2 oz) **milk chocolate**,
   melted, for drizzling

Cut the pastry into 6 pieces, then roll each piece out thinly on a lightly floured surface until a little larger than a buttered 10 cm (4 inch) individual fluted loose-bottomed tart tin. Press the pastry over the base and sides, then trim with scissors to a little above the top of the tin. Repeat until 6 tart cases have been made. Put on a baking sheet, prick the bases with a fork, then chill for 15 minutes. Bake the tarts blind (see page 15) for 8 minutes, remove the paper and beans and cook for a further 4 minutes until golden. Leave to cool.

Melt the dark chocolate and butter in a bowl set over a saucepan of gently simmering water, making sure that the water does not touch the base of the bowl. Stir in the egg yolks, one by one, then take the bowl off the heat and stir in 6 tablespoons of the cream and the sugar.

Whisk the egg whites until they form soft peaks, then fold a tablespoon into the chocolate mixture to loosen it. Add the remaining egg whites and fold in gently. Pour into the baked tart cases and chill for 3 hours until set.

Melt the white chocolate in a bowl over hot water as above. Remove the tarts from the tins and transfer to serving plates. Whip the remaining cream until it forms soft swirls, fold in the white chocolate and liqueur, then spoon on to the tarts. Drizzle with the milk chocolate and leave to stand for 10 minutes before serving.

For double chocolate & orange tarts, add the grated rind of 1 orange to the pastry. Make and bake the tarts as above, then fill with the chocolate mousse. When set, top with white chocolate cream flavoured with 4 teaspoons Grand Marnier or Cointreau.

apricot tartlets

Serves **4**
Preparation time **15 minutes**
Cooking time **20–25 minutes**

375 g (12 oz) **ready-rolled puff pastry**, defrosted if frozen
100 g (3½ oz) **marzipan**
12 **canned apricot halves**, drained
light muscovado sugar, for sprinkling
apricot jam, to glaze

Cut 4 circles from the pastry using a saucer as a template, each approximately 8 cm (3½ inches) in diameter. Score a line about 1 cm (½ inch) from the edge of each circle with a sharp knife.

Roll out the marzipan to 5 mm (¼ inch) thick and cut out 4 rounds to fit inside the scored circles. Lay the pastry rounds on a baking sheet, place a circle of marzipan in the centre of each and arrange 3 apricot halves, cut-side up, on top. Sprinkle a little sugar into each apricot.

Put the baking sheet on top of a second preheated baking sheet (this helps to crisp the pastry bases) and bake in a preheated oven, 200°C (400°F), Gas Mark 6, for 20–25 minutes until the pastry is puffed and browned and the apricots are slightly caramelized around the edges. While still hot, brush the tops with apricot jam to glaze. Serve immediately.

For banana tartlets with rum mascarpone, follow the recipe above, but use 2 thickly sliced bananas in place of the apricots. While the tartlets are baking, in a bowl, mix together 4 tablespoons mascarpone cheese, 2 tablespoons rum and 2 tablespoons light muscovado sugar. Spoon on top of the hot tartlets and serve immediately.

tarte tatin with mulled pears

Serves **6**
Preparation time **30 minutes**,
  plus cooling
Cooking time **45 minutes**

50 g (2 oz) **butter**
150 g (5 oz) **caster sugar**
200 ml (7 fl oz) **red wine**
1 **cinnamon stick**, broken in
  half
2 **star anise**
3 **cloves**
6 **conference pears**, about
  750 g (1½ lb), halved,
  peeled and cored
few drops of **red food
  colouring** (optional)
250 g (8 oz) **ready-made puff
  pastry**, defrosted if frozen

Melt the butter in a large frying pan, add the sugar, wine and spices and heat gently until the sugar has dissolved.

Add the pears to the red wine mix and simmer until the pears are almost tender (about 5 minutes), turning until evenly coloured. Scoop out of the pan and set aside.

Increase the heat and simmer the mixture for 5 minutes or until it is reduced and syrupy. Turn the heat off, stir in the food colouring, if using, then return the pears to the pan and coat in the syrup. Leave to cool for 15 minutes.

Roll out the pastry on a lightly floured surface, then trim to a 25 cm (10 inch) circle. Tip the pears, syrup and spices into a buttered metal pie dish, 20 cm (8 inches) in diameter and 5 cm (2 inches) deep. Lay the pastry on top, tucking it down the sides of the tin. Make 4 small steam vents in the top with a knife, then bake (unglazed) in a preheated oven, 200°C (400°F), Gas Mark 6, for 30 minutes until the pastry is risen, has shrunk from the sides of the tin and the juices are bubbling.

Leave to stand for 5 minutes. Loosen the edges with a knife, cover with a large serving plate, then invert the tin.

For apple tarte tatin with calvados, heat 75 g (3 oz) butter in a frying pan with 175 g (6 oz) caster sugar until the sugar has dissolved, then increase the heat and cook for 3–5 minutes, without stirring, until golden. Meanwhile, quarter, core and peel 6 firm apples, toss in the juice of 1 lemon, add to the syrup and cook very gently for 10 minutes. Cool, add to the pie dish, cover with pastry and bake as above. Turn out, and serve topped with 4 tablespoons warmed calvados flamed with a match.

italian ricotta tarts

Makes **12**

Preparation time **20 minutes**,
Cooking time **15–20 minutes**

250 g (8 oz) **ready-made puff
pastry**, defrosted if frozen
125 g (4 oz) **ricotta cheese**
1 **egg**
25 g (1 oz) **caster sugar**
grated rind of ½ **orange**
1 tablespoon chopped
candied peel
50 g (2 oz) **plain dark
chocolate**, diced
50 g (2 oz) **ready-to-eat
dried apricots**, diced
50 g (2 oz) **glacé cherries**,
chopped
sifted **icing sugar**, for dusting

Roll out the pastry thinly on a lightly floured surface,
then stamp out 12 × 8 cm (3¼ inch) circles with a
plain biscuit cutter and press into a buttered 12-section
bun tin. Prick the base of each 2–3 times with a fork.

Mix the ricotta, egg and sugar together in a bowl until
smooth, then stir in the orange rind, candied peel, diced
chocolate and fruit.

Spoon into the pastry cases and bake in a preheated
oven, 190°C (375°F), Gas Mark 5, for 15–20 minutes
until well risen and the tops of the tarts are golden.
Leave to stand for 5 minutes, then loosen the edges
with a knife and transfer to a wire rack. Dust with icing
sugar and leave to cool before serving.

For Yorkshire curd tarts, mix 125 g (4 oz) curd
cheese with 1 egg and 25 g (1 oz) caster sugar, then
stir in the grated rind of 1 lemon, 2 tablespoons
chopped candied peel and 100 g (3½ oz) sultanas.
Bake as above, then dust with icing sugar.

cherry frangipane tart

Serves **8**

Preparation time **35 minutes**, plus chilling

Cooking time **50 minutes**

450 g (14½ oz) chilled ready-made or homemade **sweet shortcrust pastry** (see page 10)

250 g (8 oz) **fresh cherries**, pitted, or a 425 g (14 oz) can, drained

3 **eggs**

100 g (3½ oz) **caster sugar**

75 g (3 oz) **unsalted butter**, melted

few drops of **almond essence**

100 g (3½ oz) **ground almonds**

2 tablespoons **flaked almonds**

sifted **icing sugar**, for dusting

Roll out the pastry on a lightly floured surface until large enough to line a buttered 25 cm (10 inch) deep-fluted, loose-bottomed tart tin. Lift the pastry over a rolling pin, drape into the tin and press it over the base and sides. Trim off excess pastry with scissors so that it stands a little above the top of the tin. Prick the base of the tart with a fork, then chill for 15 minutes.

Line the pastry with nonstick baking paper, add baking beans and bake blind in a preheated oven, 190°C (375°F), Gas Mark 5, for 15 minutes. Remove the paper and macaroni or beans and cook for a further 5 minutes. Reduce the oven temperature to 180°C (350°F), Gas Mark 4

Arrange the cherries in the base of the tart. Whisk the eggs and sugar together until thick and the whisk leaves a trail when lifted out of the mixture. Gently fold in the melted butter and almond essence, then the ground almonds. Pour the mixture over the cherries and sprinkle with the flaked almonds.

Cook the tart for 30 minutes until golden brown and the filling is set. Check after 20 minutes and cover the top loosely with foil if the tart seems to be browning too quickly.

Leave to cool in the tin for 30 minutes, then remove and dust with sifted icing sugar before serving.

For Bakewell tart, make the tart case and bake blind as above, then spread 4 tablespoons strawberry or raspberry jam over the base. Add the almond mixture and flaked almonds and bake as above.

glazed linzer torte

Serves **8**

Preparation time **30 minutes**,
   plus chilling and cooling

Cooking time **25–30 minutes**

200 g (7 oz) **redcurrants**,
   strings removed

juice of ½ **lemon**

100 g (3½ oz) **caster sugar**

2 tablespoons **cornflour**,
   mixed with a little water to
   form a paste

300 g (10 oz) **raspberries**

1 tablespoon **redcurrant jelly**

For the pastry

175 g (6 oz) **plain flour**

100 g (3½ oz) **butter**, diced

40 g (1½ oz) **icing sugar**

40 g (1½ oz) **ground
   almonds**

grated rind of **1** **lemon**

2 **egg yolks**

Add the flour and butter to a bowl and rub in with your fingertips or an electric mixer until you have fine crumbs. Stir in the icing sugar, almonds and lemon rind, then the egg yolks, and mix to form a dough. Chill for 15 minutes.

Knead the pastry, then cut off and reserve a quarter. Roll out the remainder thinly on a lightly floured surface to fit a buttered 24 cm (9½ inch) fluted loose-bottomed tart tin. Press the pastry over the base and sides of the tin. Trim off the excess and add the trimmings to the reserved pastry. Chill the tart and trimmings for 15 minutes.

Add the redcurrants, lemon juice and sugar to a pan and simmer for 5 minutes until the redcurrants are soft. Stir in the cornflour paste and cook over a high heat, stirring until the fruit compote thickens. Leave to cool.

Spread the redcurrant compote over the tart base, then sprinkle the raspberries over the top. Brush the pastry edge with water. Roll out the trimmings and cut into 1 cm (½ inch) wide strips and arrange as a lattice over the tart, pressing the edges but not trimming off the excess.

Bake the tart on a baking sheet in a preheated oven, 190°C (375°F), Gas Mark 5, for 25–30 minutes until the pastry is golden and the base is cooked. Trim off the excess pastry from the lattice. Warm the redcurrant jelly in a small pan on the hob or in the microwave and brush over the pastry lattice, then leave to cool. Remove the tart from the tin, transfer to a serving plate and serve.

For blackberry tart, make the tart as above, adding blackcurrants instead of redcurrants for the compote, and finishing with blackberries instead of raspberries. Dust with icing sugar instead of the redcurrant glaze.

blueberry & lime tarts

Makes **6**
Preparation time **30 minutes**,
  plus chilling and cooling
Cooking time **14–15 minutes**

1 quantity **pâte sucrée** (see
  page 11), chilled
150 ml (¼ pint) **double
  cream**
200 g (7 oz) **full-fat canned
  condensed milk**, chilled
grated rind of 2 **limes**
and 4 tablespoons **lime juice**
1 tablespoon **cornflour**
1 tablespoon **water**
200 g (7 oz) **blueberries**
50 g (2 oz) **caster sugar**

Cut the pastry into 6 pieces, then roll each piece out thinly on a lightly floured surface until a little larger than a buttered 10 cm (4 inch) fluted loose-bottomed tart tin. Lift into the tins, press over the base and sides, then trim the excess pastry with scissors so it stands a little above the top of the tin. Put on a baking sheet, prick the bases with a fork, then chill for 15 minutes.

Line the tarts with nonstick baking paper and baking beans and bake blind in a preheated oven, 190°C (375°F), Gas Mark 5 for 8 minutes, then remove the paper and beans and cook for a further 4 minutes until golden. Leave to cool.

Whisk the cream in a bowl until it foms soft swirls. Add the condensed milk and lime rind and whisk to mix. Gradually whisk in the lime juice until thick. Spoon into the tart cases and chill until ready to serve.

Mix the cornflour and the measurement water to a smooth paste in the base of a small saucepan, add the blueberries and sugar and cook for 2–3 minutes until the blueberries just begin to soften and the juices run. Leave to cool.

When ready to serve, remove the tarts from the tins and spoon the blueberry compote on top.

For Florida lime tarts, make up the tart cases as above. Fill with the condensed milk, lime juice and cream mixture, but reserve the lime rind. Chill as above. Top with 150 ml (¼ pint) whipped double cream and sprinkle with the reserved lime rind.

candied orange & chocolate tart

Serves **8**

Preparation time **35 minutes**, plus chilling and cooling

Cooking time **1¼ hours**

200 g (7 oz) **caster sugar**

4 tablespoons **water**

2 medium **oranges**, thinly sliced

1 quantity **all-butter sweet shortcrust pastry** (see page 10)

100 g (3½ oz) **butter**, at room temperature

100 g (3½ oz) **ground almonds**

2 **eggs**, beaten

100 g (3½ oz) **plain dark chocolate**, melted

Add half the sugar and the water to a saucepan and heat gently until the sugar has dissolved. Add the orange slices and cook over a low heat for 30 minutes until the oranges are tender, the peel is soft and almost translucent and most of the syrup has evaporated. Cool.

Roll the pastry out thinly on a lightly floured surface to fit a buttered 24 cm (9½ inch) fluted loose-bottomed tart tin. Press the pastry over the base and sides of the tin. Trim off the excess with scissors so that it stands a little above the top of the tin. Chill for 15 minutes.

Bake the tart blind (see page 15) for 10 minutes. Remove the paper and baking beans and cook for a further 5 minutes. Remove from the oven and reduce the oven temperature to 180°C (350°F), Gas Mark 4.

Cream the butter and the remaining sugar in a bowl until light and fluffy. Add the ground almonds, gradually beat in the eggs until smooth, then set aside.

Reserve 10 of the best orange slices for decoration, then drain and chop the rest. Stir the melted chocolate into the almond mixture, then mix in the chopped oranges. Spread into the tart case, arrange the reserved orange slices in a ring on top and bake for 30 minutes. Leave to cool for 30 minutes before removing from the tin.

For pear & chocolate tart, make up the almond mix as above, stir in the melted chocolate, then add 4 teaspoons finely chopped glacé ginger in place of the chopped orange. Spread it in the tart case, then peel, core and slice 2 pears and press these on top. Sprinkle with 2 tablespoons flaked almonds. Bake as above, then sprinkle with diced chocolate when out of the oven.

gingered treacle tart

Serves **8**
Preparation time **30 minutes**
Cooking time **45–55 minutes**

680 g (1 lb 6 oz) jar **golden syrup**
25 g (1 oz) **butter**
juice of 1 **lemon**
125 g (4 oz) **fresh breadcrumbs**
50 g (2 oz) **glacé** or **stem ginger**, drained and chopped
2 **Braeburn apples**, cored and coarsely grated

For the pastry
200 g (7 oz) **plain flour**
100 g (3½ oz) **butter**, diced
finely grated rind of 1 **lemon**
2 tablespoons **cold water**
milk, to glaze

Tip the golden syrup into a saucepan, add the butter and heat gently until melted. Stir in the lemon juice, breadcrumbs, ginger and apples then leave to cool.

Make the pastry. Put the flour, butter and lemon rind in a bowl and rub in the butter until you have fine crumbs. Mix in just enough of the measurement water to form a smooth dough. Knead lightly, roll out on a lightly floured surface and use to line a 24 cm (9½ inch) loose-bottomed tart tin. Trim off the excess pastry and reserve.

Pour the syrup mixture into the tart case. Roll out the pastry trimmings thinly, cut narrow strips and arrange in a lattice, sticking the edges with a little milk. Brush all the strips with milk.

Place the tart on a hot baking sheet and bake in a preheated oven, 190°C (375°F), Gas Mark 5, for 40–50 minutes until golden and the filling has set. Check after 30 minutes and cover the top loosely with foil if the tart seems to be browning too quickly.

Serve warm or cold with clotted cream or ice cream.

For pecan pie, make up the tart case as above. Warm 175 g (6 oz) golden syrup in a saucepan with 200 g (7 oz) light muscovado sugar and 75 g (3 oz) butter until melted. Cool slightly, then beat in 3 eggs and ½ teaspoon vanilla essence. Pour into the tart case and arrange 175 g (6 oz) pecans on top. Bake at 180°C (350°F), Gas Mark 4, for 40–50 minutes or until set, covering with foil if necessary.

pear & almond tart

Serves **8**

Preparation time **20 minutes**, plus chilling

Cooking time **50–55 minutes**

450 g (14½ oz) chilled ready-made or homemade **sweet shortcrust pastry** (see page 10)

125 g (4 oz) **unsalted butter**, at room temperature

125 g (4 oz) **caster sugar**

125 g (4 oz) **ground almonds**

2 **eggs**, lightly beaten

1 tablespoon **lemon juice**

3 **ripe pears**, peeled, cored and thickly sliced

25 g (1 oz) **flaked almonds**

sifted **icing sugar**, for dusting

Roll out the pastry on a lightly floured surface until a little larger than a 25 cm (10 inch) tart tin. Lift the pastry over a rolling pin, drape into the tin, then press over the base and sides. Trim off excess pastry with scissors so that it stands a little above the top of the tin. Prick the base with a fork and chill for 30 minutes.

Line the tart with nonstick baking paper, add baking beans and bake in a preheated oven, 190°C (375°F), Gas Mark 5, for 15 minutes. Remove the baking paper and beans and bake for a further 5–10 minutes until the pastry is crisp and golden. Leave to cool completely. Reduce the oven temperature to 180°C (350°F), Gas Mark 4.

Beat the butter, sugar and ground almonds together until smooth, then beat in the eggs and lemon juice.

Arrange the pear slices over the pastry case and carefully spread over the almond mixture. Sprinkle with the flaked almonds and bake for 30 minutes until the topping is golden and firm to the touch. Remove from the oven and leave to cool.

Dust the tart with sifted icing sugar and serve in wedges with chocolate sauce (see below) and some vanilla ice cream.

For chocolate sauce, to serve as an accompaniment, melt 100 g (3½ oz) plain dark chocolate, broken into pieces with 50 g (2 oz) unsalted butter, diced, and 1 tablespoon golden syrup in a saucepan over a gentle heat. Leave to cool slightly.

toffeed apple tarts

Makes **12**
Preparation time **40 minutes**,
  plus chilling
Cooking time **20 minutes**

1 quantity **pâte sucrée** (see
  page 11), chilled
2 teaspoons **cornflour**
2 tablespoons **water**
750 g (1½ lb) **dessert
  apples**, cored, peeled and
  diced
100 g (3½ oz) **light
  muscovado sugar**
25 g (1 oz) **butter**

For the topping
250 ml (8 fl oz) **double cream**
3 tablespoons **light
  muscovado sugar**

Roll the pastry out thinly on a lightly floured surface,
then stamp out 12 × 10 cm (4 inch) circles with a fluted
biscuit cutter and press into a buttered 12-section
muffin tin, rerolling the pastry trimmings as needed.
Prick the bases 2–3 times, then chill for 15 minutes.

Bake the tarts blind (see page 15) for 5 minutes.
Remove the paper and baking beans and cook for a
further 4–5 minutes until pale golden. Remove from the
oven, and reduce the oven temperature to 180°C
(350°F), Gas Mark 4.

Meanwhile, mix the cornflour and the measurement
water to a paste in a saucepan, add the apples, sugar
and cook for 10 minutes, stirring from time to time, until
the butter and apples are soft. Leave to cool for 15
minutes, then loosen the tarts and remove from the tin.

Spoon the apples into the tart cases. Whip the cream
to form soft swirls. Fold in 2 tablespoons sugar, spoon
over the tarts and sprinkle with the remaining sugar.
Serve cold.

For toffee marshmallow tarts, make the tart cases
and filling as above. Whisk 3 egg whites until stiff,
then gradually whisk in 50 g (2 oz) caster sugar and
50 g (2 oz) light muscovado sugar until the meringue
is thick and glossy. Spoon over the apple-filled tarts,
then bake in a preheated oven, 160°C (325°F), Gas
Mark 3, for 15 minutes until browned.

double chocolate tart

Serves **6–8**
Preparation time **40 minutes**,
  plus chilling and cooling
Cooking time **40 minutes**

400 g (13 oz) chilled **ready-made** or **homemade sweet shortcrust pastry** (see page 10)
150 g (5 oz) **plain dark chocolate**, broken into pieces, plus 50 g (2 oz) to decorate
150 g (5 oz) **white chocolate**
100 g (3½ oz) **unsalted butter**
3 **eggs**
1 **egg yolk**
100 g (3½ oz) **caster sugar**
2 tablespoons **double cream**

Roll out the pastry on a lightly floured surface until large enough to line a buttered 24 cm (9½ inch) fluted, loose-bottomed flan tin. Lift over a rolling pin, drape into the tin and press over the base and sides. Trim off the excess pastry, prick the base with a fork, then chill for 15 minutes. Line with nonstick baking paper, add baking beans and bake in a preheated oven, 190°C (375°F), Gas Mark 5, for 15 minutes. Remove the paper and beans and bake for a further 5 minutes. Remove from the oven and reduce the oven temperature to 160°C (325°F), Gas Mark 3.

Melt the dark and white chocolate in separate bowls over a saucepan of simmering water. Add three-quarters of the butter to the dark chocolate and the rest to the white chocolate. Leave until melted.

Whisk the eggs, egg yolk and sugar in a third bowl for 3–4 minutes until doubled in volume (but not so thick as to leave a trail). Fold two-thirds into the dark chocolate mixture, then pour into the cooked tart case. Fold the cream into the white chocolate to loosen it, then fold in the remaining whisked egg mixture. Spoon over the dark chocolate layer to completely cover. Cook the tart for 20 minutes until just set with a slight wobble to the centre. Cool for at least 1 hour. Pipe double lines of melted dark chocolate and leave for at least 30 minutes before serving.

For dark chocolate tart, melt 300 g (10 oz) plain dark chocolate with 100 g (3½ oz) butter. Whisk the eggs and sugar as above and fold into the chocolate mixture. Pour into the baked tart case and cook for 15 minutes. Dust with sifted cocoa to serve.

mango & palm sugar tatin

Serves **8**

Preparation time **40 minutes**,
  plus freezing

Cooking time **20–25 minutes**

75 g (3 oz) **unsalted butter**

75 g (3 oz) **palm sugar**,
  grated, or **light soft brown
  sugar**

½ teaspoon ground **mixed
  spice**

3 small **mangoes**, peeled,
  pitted and thickly sliced

350 g (12 oz) chilled **ready-
  made puff pastry** or
  homemade flaky pastry

Make the topping. Heat the butter, sugar and spice together in a 23 cm (9 inch) ovenproof frying pan until the butter has melted. Remove the pan from the heat. Carefully arrange the mango slices in the pan, fanning them from the centre outwards, to make 2 layers.

Roll out the pastry on a lightly floured surface a little larger than the size of the pan. Drape it over the mangoes and press it down and around the edges of the pan, then pierce a small hole in the centre. Bake in a preheated oven, 220°C (425°F), Gas Mark 7, for 20–25 minutes until the pastry is risen and golden. Leave to stand for 10 minutes before turning out on to a large plate. Serve with ice cream.

For coconut ice cream, to accompany the tatin, bring 300 ml (½ pint) full-fat milk, 400 ml (14 fl oz) can full-fat coconut milk and 2 star anise just to the boil in a saucepan. Take off the heat and leave to infuse for 20 minutes, then strain. Beat 5 egg yolks with 75 g (3 oz) caster sugar until pale and creamy. Stir in the cream mix, then pour back into the pan and heat gently, stirring until it coats the back of the spoon. Cool, then freeze in an electric ice-cream machine until thick or in a plastic box in the freezer, beating several times until firm.

summer berry tarts

Makes **12**
Preparation time **30 minutes**,
  plus chilling
Cooking time **12 minutes**

1 quantity **pâte sucrée** (see
  page 11), chilled
300 ml (½ pint) **double
  cream**
4 tablespoons **lemon curd**
3 tablespoons **redcurrant jelly**
juice of ½ **lemon**
250 g (8 oz) small
  strawberries, halved or
  sliced depending on size
200 g (7 oz) **raspberries**
150 g (5 oz) **blueberries**

Roll the pastry out thinly on a lightly floured surface, then stamp out 12 × 10 cm (4 inch) circles with a fluted biscuit cutter and press into a buttered 12-section muffin tin. Reknead and reroll the pastry trimmings as needed. Prick the bases 2–3 times with a fork, then chill for 15 minutes.

Line the tarts with small squares of nonstick baking paper and baking beans and bake in a preheated oven, 190°C (375°F), Gas Mark 5, for 8 minutes. Remove the paper and beans and cook for a further 4–5 minutes until golden. Leave to cool for 10 minutes, then loosen the edges and transfer to a wire rack to cool completely.

Whip the cream until it forms soft swirls, then fold in the lemon curd. Spoon into the tart cases and spread into an even layer with the back of a teaspoon.

Warm the redcurrant jelly and lemon juice together in a small saucepan, stirring, until the jelly has dissolved completely. Add the fruits and toss together. Spoon over the tarts, piling the fruit up high, then transfer to a serving plate.

For summer berry & white chocolate tarts, omit the lemon curd from the cream and fold in 125 g (4 oz) melted white chocolate instead. Spoon into the tarts, arrange the raw fruits on top without the redcurrant glaze, then drizzle 75 g (3 oz) melted white chocolate in lines over the fruit.

pecan, maple syrup & choc tart

Serves **8**
Preparation time **20 minutes**,
  plus chilling and cooling
Cooking time **1 hour**
  10 minutes

125 g (4 oz) **unsalted butter**,
  at room temperature
125 g (4 oz) **light soft brown**
  sugar
2 **eggs**, beaten
4 tablespoons **plain flour**
pinch of **salt**
175 ml (6 fl oz) **maple syrup**
175 g (6 oz) **pecan nuts**,
  toasted
100 g (3½ oz) **pine nuts**,
  lightly toasted
50 g (2 oz) **plain dark**
  chocolate, chopped

For the pastry
200 g (7 oz) **plain flour**, sifted
¼ teaspoon **salt**
100 g (3½ oz) **unsalted**
  butter, diced
1 **egg**, lightly beaten
2–3 teaspoons **cold water**

Make the pastry. Add the flour, salt and butter to a bowl, then rub the butter in with your fingertips or an electric mixer until you have fine crumbs. Add the egg and water and continue mixing until the pastry just starts to come together. Transfer to a lightly floured surface, knead gently. Wrap the dough in clingfilm and chill for 30 minutes.

Roll out the dough thinly on a lightly floured surface and use it to line a 23 cm (9 inch) square flan tin (see page 14). Prick the base with a fork and chill for 20 minutes. Line the tart case with nonstick baking paper, add baking beans and bake blind in a preheated oven, 190°C (375°F), Gas Mark 5, for 15 minutes. Remove the paper and baking beans and bake for a further 5–10 minutes until crisp and golden. Leave to cool. Reduce the oven temperature to 180°C (350°F), Gas Mark 4.

Cream the butter and sugar until pale and light, then gradually beat in the eggs, adding the flour and salt as you go until evenly combined. Stir in the syrup (the mixture may appear to curdle at this stage), nuts and chocolate and spoon the mixture into the pastry case.

Bake for 40–45 minutes until golden and just firm in the centre. Remove from the oven and leave to cool. Serve warm with ice cream.

For traditional pecan pie, add a large pinch of ground mixed spice in the pastry. Use 250 g (8 oz) pecan nuts and omit the pine nuts and chocolate, flavouring with 1 teaspoon vanilla extract instead.

kaffir lime tart

Serves **8**

Preparation time **20 minutes**, plus chilling

Cooking time **33–40 minutes**

400 g (13 oz) chilled ready-made or homemade **sweet shortcrust pastry** (see page 10)

a little **flour**, for dusting

175 g (6 oz) **caster sugar**

200 ml (7 fl oz) freshly squeezed **lime juice** (4–6 limes)

8 **kaffir lime leaves** or the grated rind of 3 **limes**

3 **eggs**

2 **egg yolks**

175 g (6 oz) **unsalted butter**, at room temperature

sifted **icing sugar**, for dusting

Roll out the pastry on a lightly floured surface a little larger than a 23 cm (9 inch) fluted flan tin. Lift the pastry over a rollng pin, drape into the tin and press over the base and sides. Trim off any excess pastry, and prick the base with a fork. Chill for 30 minutes.

Line the tart with nonstick baking paper, add baking beans and bake in a preheated oven, 200°C (400°F), Gas Mark 6, for 15 minutes. Remove the paper and beans and bake for a further 12–15 minutes until the pastry is crisp and golden. Leave to cool.

Put the sugar, lime juice and kaffir lime leaves or lime rind in a saucepan and heat gently to dissolve the sugar. Bring to the boil and simmer for 5 minutes. Leave to cool for 5 minutes, then strain into a clean pan.

Stir in the eggs, egg yolks and half the butter and heat gently, stirring, for 1 minute or until the sauce coats the back of the spoon. Add the remaining butter and whisk constantly until the mixture thickens.

Transfer the lime mixture to the pastry case and bake for 6–8 minutes until set. Leave to cool and serve warm dusted with icing sugar.

For mango & kiwifruit salad, to serve with the tart, peel, stone and dice 1 large mango, then mix with 3 peeled and sliced kiwifruits, the seeds scooped from 3 passion fruits and the juice of 1 lime.

macadamia & vanilla tart

Serves **8-10**
Preparation time **30 minutes**
Cooking time **45 minutes**

400 g (13 oz) chilled ready-
   made or homemade **sweet
   shortcrust pastry** (see
   page 10)
75 g (3 oz) **light brown sugar**
150 ml (¼ pint) **maple syrup**
75 g (3 oz) **unsalted butter**
1 teaspoon **vanilla extract**
150 g (5 oz) **ground almonds**
4 **eggs**, beaten
200 g (7 oz) **macadamia
   nuts**, coarsely chopped

Roll out the pastry thinly on a lightly floured surface a little larger than a 23 cm (9 inch) loose-bottomed baking tin. Lift the pastry over a rollng pin, drape into the tin and press over the base and sides. Trim off any excess pastry, and prick the base with a fork.

Line the tart with nonstick baking paper, add baking beans and bake in a preheated oven, 190°C (375°F), Gas Mark 5, for 15 minutes. Remove the paper and beans and bake for a further 5 minutes. Remove from the oven and reduce the oven temperature to 160°C (325°F), Gas Mark 3.

Heat the sugar, maple syrup and butter gently until melted. Remove from the heat and beat in the vanilla essence and ground almonds, followed by the eggs. Add half the macadamia nuts and turn the mix into the pastry case.

Sprinkle with the remaining macadamia nuts and bake for about 25 minutes or until the filling forms a crust but remains quite soft underneath. Leave to cool for 10 minutes, then serve with ice cream or cream.

For pine nut & honey tart, make and bake the tart case as above. Cream together 100 g (3½ oz) unsalted butter with 100 g (3½ oz) caster sugar. Beat in 3 eggs, one at a time, then mix in 175 g (6 oz) warmed flower honey, the grated rind and juice of 1 lemon and 200 g (7 oz) pine nuts. Pour into the tart case and bake in a preheated oven, 180°C (350°F), Gas Mark 4, for about 40 minutes until browned and set.

honeyed pecan pie

Serves **8**

Preparation time **30 minutes**, plus chilling

Cooking time **40–45 minutes**

1 quantity **all-butter sweet shortcrust pastry** (see page 10)

200 g (7oz) **runny honey**

200 g (7oz) **light muscovado sugar**

75 g (3 oz) **butter**

¼ teaspoon **ground cinnamon**

1 teaspoon **vanilla extract**

3 **eggs**

150 g (5 oz) **pecan nuts**

Roll the pastry out thinly on a lightly floured surface until a little larger than a buttered fluted loose-bottomed flan tin, 23 cm (9 inches) in diameter and 2.5 cm (1 inch) deep. Line the tin (see page 14). Trim off the excess pastry with scissors so that it stands a little above the top of the tin. Prick the base with a fork, then chill for 15 minutes.

Line the pastry case with nonstick baking paper and baking beans and bake blind (see page 15) for 10 minutes. Remove the paper and beans and cook for a further 5 minutes until the case is crisp. Remove from the oven, and reduce the oven temperature to 180°C (350°F), Gas Mark 4.

Meanwhile, put the honey, sugar, butter and cinnamon into a saucepan and heat gently, stirring occasionally, until melted. Take off the heat and leave to cool slightly.

Beat the vanilla with the eggs in a small jug, then gradually beat into the cooled honey mixture. Pour into the pastry case and arrange the nuts over the top. Carefully transfer to the oven and bake for 25–30 minutes until the filling is set and the nuts have darkened. Check after 15 minutes and cover the top loosely with foil if the top seems to be browning too quickly.

Leave to cool in the tin for 30 minutes before serving with scoops of vanilla ice cream.

For chocolate pecan pie, reduce the amount of honey and sugar to 150 g (5 oz) each, heat with the butter and cinnamon until the butter has melted, then take off the heat and add 100 g (3½ oz) plain dark chocolate, broken into pieces. Leave to stand for 5 minutes until the chocolate has melted, then continue as above.

brandied prune & custard tart

Serves **8**
Preparation time **30 minutes**,
  plus standing and chilling
Cooking time **45–50 minutes**

4 tablespoons **brandy**
250 g (8 oz) **ready-to-eat
  pitted prunes**
150 ml (¼ pint) **double
  cream**
150 ml (¼ pint) **milk**
1 **vanilla pod**, slit in half
  lengthways
1 quantity **pâte sucrée** (see
  page 11), chilled
4 **eggs**
50 g (2 oz) **caster sugar**
sifted **icing sugar**, for dusting

Warm the brandy in a saucepan, add the prunes, simmer gently for 3–4 minutes, then take off the heat. Pour the cream and milk into a second saucepan, add the vanilla pod and bring just to the boil, then take off the heat. Cover both pans and set aside for 2 hours.

Meanwhile, roll the pastry out on a lightly floured surface to fit a buttered 24 cm (9½ inch) fluted loose-bottomed tart tin, then press the pastry over the base and sides. Trim off the excess pastry with scissors so that it stands a little above the top of the tin. Prick the base with a fork and chill for 15 minutes.

Bake the tart case blind (see page 15) for 10 minutes. Remove the paper and baking beans and bake for a further 5 minutes. Remove from the oven and reduce the oven temperature to 180°C (350°F), Gas Mark 4.

Whisk the eggs and sugar together in a large bowl until creamy. Retrieve the vanilla pod, scrape out the seeds and add the seeds to the eggs, then whisk in the milk mixture.

Drain the prunes, adding excess brandy to the milk mix, then arrange in the base of the tart case. Pour over the custard and bake for 25–30 minutes until the custard is pale golden and just set. Leave to cool, then remove from the tin and dust with icing sugar to serve.

For apricot & orange custard tart, make up the tart case as above. Simmer 200 g (7 oz) halved dried apricots in the juice of 1 orange and 4 tablespoons water for 5 minutes. Set aside for 2 hours. Add the grated rind of ½ orange to the custard and make as above. Arrange the apricots in the tart case, pour over the custard and bake as above.

206

caramel & chocolate tart

Serves **8**

Preparation time **30 minutes**, plus chilling and cooling

Cooking time **20 minutes**

1 quantity **pâte sucrée** (see page 11), chilled

100 g (3½ oz) **butter**

100 g (3½ oz) **dark muscovado sugar**

400 g (13 oz) **full-fat condensed milk**

75 g (3 oz) **plain dark chocolate**, broken into pieces

75 g (3 oz) **white chocolate**, broken into pieces

Roll the pastry out thinly on a lightly floured surface until a little larger than a buttered 22 cm (8½ inch) loose-bottomed fluted tart tin. Line the tin (see page 14). Trim off the excess pastry with scissors so that it stands a little above the top of the tin. Prick the base with a fork, then chill for 15 minutes.

Bake the tart blind (see page 15) for 10 minutes. Remove the paper and beans and cook for a further 5–10 minutes or until crisp. Leave to cool completely.

Heat the butter and sugar in a saucepan until the butter has melted and the sugar dissolved. Add the condensed milk and cook over a low heat, stirring for 4–5 minutes until just beginning to darken and smell of caramel. Pour into the tart case, spread evenly and leave to cool.

Melt the dark and white chocolate in separate bowls set over two small saucepans of just simmering water, making sure that the water does not touch the base of the bowls.

Remove the tart from the tin and transfer to a serving plate. Drizzle random spoonfuls of plain dark chocolate over the pie. Cool for 10 minutes, then drizzle random spoonfuls of melted white chocolate over the dark layer. Leave to set. Cut into thin wedges to serve.

For caramel & banana cream tart, fill the tart with caramel filling as above, then cool. Whip 300 ml (½ pint) double cream and fold in 2 small sliced bananas that have been tossed in the juice of ½ lemon. Spoon over the top of the tart and sprinkle with a little grated plain dark chocolate.

ginger tarts & coconut rum cream

Makes **12**
Preparation time **30 minutes**,
plus chilling and cooling
Cooking time **19–23 minutes**

1 quantity **pâte sucrée** (see
page 11), chilled
25 g (1 oz) **butter**
125 g (4 oz) **light muscovado
sugar**
125 g (4 oz) **golden syrup**
3 **eggs**, beaten
1 teaspoon **ground ginger**
4 teaspoons chopped **glacé**
or **stem ginger**
1 **banana**
grated rind and juice of 1 **lime**

For the coconut rum cream
300 ml (½ pint) **double
cream**
2 tablespoons **icing sugar**
4 tablespoons **white** or **dark
rum**
4 tablespoons **desiccated
coconut**, plus extra for
sprinkling

Roll the pastry out thinly on a lightly floured surface,
then stamp out 12 × 10 cm (4 inch) circles with a
fluted biscuit cutter and press into a buttered 12-
section muffin tin, rerolling the pastry trimmings as
needed. Prick the bases of each tart 2–3 times with a
fork, then chill for 15 minutes.

Bake the tarts blind (see page 15) for 5 minutes.
Remove the paper and beans and cook for a further
2–3 minutes. Remove from the oven, and reduce the
oven temperature to 180°C (350°F), Gas Mark 4.

Add the butter, sugar and syrup to a medium saucepan
and heat gently until the butter has just melted, then
leave to cool slightly. Beat in the eggs, then the ground
and chopped ginger. Spoon into the tart cases and
bake for 12–15 minutes. Leave to cool in the tins – the
filling will sink and firm up as it cools.

Loosen the tarts with a knife, lift out of the tin and put
on a wire rack, if still warm, or a plate if cold. Make the
coconut rum cream by whipping the cream and icing
sugar together until it forms soft swirls, then fold in the
rum and coconut. Spoon over the top of the tarts.

Peel and slice the banana, then toss with the lime juice.
Arrange slices at angles in the cream and sprinkle with
lime rind a little extra coconut.

For chocolate tarts & coconut rum cream, omit the
ground ginger and chopped ginger from the filling,
adding 75 g (3 oz) plain dark chocolate when melting
the butter. Add the grated rind of 1 orange to the
whipped cream and rum mix and omit the banana.

white choc & cranberry tart

Makes **6**

Preparation time **30 minutes**,
  plus cooling and chilling

Cooking time **20 minutes**

250 g (8 oz) **frozen
  cranberries**

50 g (2 oz) **golden caster
  sugar**

4 tablespoons **crème de
  cassis**

200 g (7 oz) **white chocolate**,
  broken into pieces

300 g (10 oz) **fat-free
  fromage frais**

1 teaspoon **vanilla extract**

2 tablespoons **cranberry jelly**

6 **ready-made all-butter
  pastry cases**

Gently heat the cranberries, sugar and crème de cassis in a saucepan for a few minutes until the cranberries are just softened. Strain the cranberries and set aside to cool, reserving the juice.

Melt the white chocolate in a bowl set over a saucepan of barely simmering water, making sure the water does not touch the base of the bowl. Stir in the fromage frais and vanilla extract and beat together well. Cover and chill.

Add the cranberry jelly to the reserved cranberry juice in the pan. Heat gently to melt the jelly and then stir to combine.

Spoon the vanilla and white chocolate mixture into the pastry cases 1–2 hours before serving. Top with the cranberries and spoon the cranberry syrup over to glaze. Chill until needed.

For homemade pastry cases, combine 175 g (6 oz) plain flour with 75 g (3 oz) butter until the mixture forms crumbs. Add 50 g (2 oz) icing sugar and 2 egg yolks and mix until a dough forms. Wrap in clingfilm and chill for 30 minutes. Grease and base-line 6 tins, 6 x 8 cm (2½ x 3¼ inches). Divide the pastry into 6, then press into the tins. Chill for 20 minutes. Trim off the excess pastry, line with nonstick baking paper and fill with baking beans, then bake in a preheated oven, 190°C (375°F), Gas Mark 5, for 8 minutes. Remove the paper and beans and cook for a further 4 minutes until golden and crisp. Cool in the tins for 10 minutes, then cool on a wire rack before using.

gluten-free

quiches lorraine

Makes **6**
Preparation time **30 minutes**,
  plus chilling
Cooking time **30–35 minutes**

1 quantity **gluten-free pastry**
  (see page 13)
1 tablespoon **sunflower oil**
4 **smoked streaky bacon
  rashers**, about 75 g (3 oz),
  diced
1 small **onion**, chopped
125 g (4 oz) **mature Cheddar
  cheese**, grated
3 **eggs**
200 ml (7 fl oz) **milk**
1 teaspoon **mustard powder**
1 tablespoon chopped **chives**
  (optional)
salt and **pepper**

Cut the pastry into 6, then roll one portion out between 2 sheets of clingfilm until a little larger than a buttered individual 10 cm (4 inch) loose-bottomed fluted tart tin. Remove the top sheet of clingfilm, turn the pastry over, drape into the tart tin and remove the top sheet of clingfilm. Press the pastry into the base and sides of the tin with fingers dusted in rice flour. Trim off the excess pastry with scissors a little above the top of the tin. Patch any cracks or breaks with pastry trimmings. Repeat until 6 tarts have been made. Put on a baking sheet and chill for 15 minutes.

Meanwhile, to make the filling, heat the oil in a frying pan, add the bacon and onion and fry for 5 minutes, stirring until golden.

Divide three-quarters of the cheese between the tart cases, then sprinkle the onion and bacon mix on top. Beat the eggs, milk and mustard in a jug with a little salt and pepper, then pour into the tarts. Sprinkle with the chives, if using, and the remaining cheese.

Bake in a preheated oven, 190°C (375°F), Gas Mark 5, for 25–30 minutes until the tops are golden and the pastry bases cooked through. Leave to cool for 5 minutes, then remove from the tins and serve with salad.

For mushroom quiches, omit the bacon, adding 125 g (4 oz) sliced button mushrooms and 25 g (1 oz) butter to the lightly fried onions, and fry for 3–4 minutes until the mushrooms are just beginning to colour. Add the cheese to the tart cases and continue as above.

cheesy picnic pies

Makes **4**
Preparation time **25 minutes**
Cooking time **35 minutes**

1 tablespoon **olive oil**
1 **onion**, chopped
2 **garlic cloves**, finely
  chopped
1 **courgette**, diced
½ **yellow pepper**, deseeded
  and diced
½ **red pepper**, deseeded and
  diced
400 g (13 oz) can **chopped
  tomatoes**
1 tablespoon chopped
  rosemary or **basil**
½ teaspoon **caster sugar**
beaten egg, to glaze
salt and **pepper**

For the pastry
175 g (6 oz) **gluten-free
  bread flour**
75 g (3 oz) **butter**, diced
75 g (3 oz) **mature Cheddar
  cheese**, diced, plus extra,
  grated, for sprinkling
2 **egg yolks**
2 teaspoons **water**

Heat the oil in a saucepan, add the onion and fry for 5 minutes until softened. Add the garlic, courgette and diced peppers and fry briefly, then add the tomatoes, herbs, sugar and a little salt and pepper. Simmer, uncovered, for 10 minutes, stirring from time to time until thickened. Cool.

Make the pastry. Add the flour, butter and a little salt and pepper to a bowl, rub in the butter until you have fine crumbs, then stir in the cheese. Add the egg yolks and water and mix to form a smooth dough.

Knead lightly, then cut the dough into 4 pieces. Roll one of the pieces out between 2 sheets of clingfilm, patting into a neat shape until you have an 18 cm (7 inch) circle. Remove the top sheet of clingfilm, spoon one-quarter of the filling in the centre, brush the pastry edges with beaten egg, then fold the pastry circle in half while still on the lower piece of clingfilm.

Peel the pastry off the film, lift on to an oiled baking sheet, press the edges together well and press together any breaks in the pastry. Repeat with the remaining pastry pieces and filling until 4 pies have been made.

Brush with beaten egg, sprinkle with a little extra cheese and bake in a preheated oven, 190°C (375°F), Gas Mark 5, for 20 minutes until golden brown. Loosen and transfer to a wire rack. Serve warm or cold with salad.

For ham & tomato picnic pies, omit the red and yellow peppers and stir 50 g (2 oz) diced ham into the tomato mixture when cold. Continue as above.

cidered chicken pie

Serves **4**

Preparation time **30 minutes**, plus cooling

Cooking time **1½–1¾ hours**

25 g (1 oz) **butter**

8 **chicken thighs on the bone**

2 **leeks**, trimmed and thickly sliced, white and green parts separated

300 ml (½ pint) **chicken stock**

300 ml (½ pint) **dry cider**

3 sprigs **thyme**, leaves torn from stems

1 tablespoon **cornflour**, mixed with a little water

125 g (4 oz) **closed-cup mushrooms**, sliced

1 quantity **gluten-free pastry** (see page 13)

beaten egg, to glaze

salt and **pepper**

Heat the butter in a frying pan, add the chicken and fry on both sides until golden. Remove from the pan and set aside. Add the white leek slices to the pan and fry for 2–3 minutes until softened. Return the chicken to the pan, add the stock, cider and thyme, then season with salt and pepper. Bring to the boil, cover and simmer for 45 minutes until the chicken is cooked through.

Transfer the chicken to a plate. Stir the cornflour mix into the stock pan and bring to the boil, stirring until thickened, then take off the heat. Remove the skin and bones from the chicken, dice the meat and add to the sauce with the green leeks and mushrooms. Leave to cool.

Spoon the filling into the base of a 1.2 litre (2 pint) pie dish. Roll out the pastry between 2 sheets of clingfilm for the lid. Brush the rim of the dish with beaten egg.

Remove one sheet of clingfilm, lay the pastry over the dish, then remove the top sheet of clingfilm. Press the pastry on to the dish with fingers dusted with rice flour. Trim off the excess, then brush with beaten egg. Bake in a preheated oven, 190°C (375°F), Gas Mark 5, for 30–35 minutes until the pastry is golden and the filling is piping hot.

For chicken & tarragon pie, fry the chicken as above, then drain and fry the white leek slices with 4 diced smoked streaky bacon rashers until golden. Add 150 ml (¼ pint) dry white wine, 450 ml (¾ pint) chicken stock, salt and pepper, omitting the thyme. Cover and simmer, thicken as above, then add the green leek slices, 1 tablespoon chopped tarragon and 2 tablespoons chopped parsley, omitting the mushrooms. Spoon into the dish and continue as above.

sausage & caramelized onion rolls

Makes **8**
Preparation time **30 minutes**
Cooking time **35–40 minutes**

1 tablespoon **olive oil**
1 **onion**, thinly sliced
1 **garlic clove**, finely chopped
1 teaspoon **caster sugar**
1 **dessert apple**, quartered,
  cored, peeled
200 g (7 oz) **minced pork**
1 **egg yolk**
8 **sage leaves**
1 quantity **gluten-free pastry**
  (see page 13)
beaten egg, to glaze
salt and **pepper**

Heat the oil in a frying pan, add the onion and fry gently for 10 minutes until softened. Add the garlic and sugar, increase the heat slightly and fry for 5 more minutes, stirring more frequently until a deep golden.

Add the apple to a food processor and finely chop. Add the pork, egg yolk, sage and plenty of salt and pepper and blitz. (Alternatively, finely chop the apple and sage, then mix with pork, egg yolk and seasoning.)

Roll out half the pastry between 2 sheets of clingfilm to a strip about 30 × 10 cm (12 × 4 inches). Remove the top clingfilm and spoon half the onion mix in a line down the centre, then spoon half the minced pork in a line on top. Brush the edges of the pastry with beaten egg.

Fold the pastry strip in half to enclose the filling and press the edges together with fingers dusted with rice flour to seal well. Trim the edges to neaten, then cut the strips into pieces about 7.5 cm (3 inches) thick. Arrange slightly spaced apart on an oiled baking sheet. Repeat with the remaining pastry, onion and pork mix.

Make 2–3 small slashes in the top of each sausage roll, brush with beaten egg to glaze, then bake in a preheated oven, 190°C (375°F), Gas Mark 5, for 20–25 minutes until the pastry is golden and the filling cooked through. Transfer to a wire rack and leave to cool.

For traditional sausage rolls, roll out half the pastry as above, arrange 3 skinned gluten-free herb sausages on top, brush the edge with egg, then fold over, seal and cut into pieces. Repeat with the remaining pastry and 3 more sausages. Cut into pieces and bake as above.

beef & mustard pies

Makes **4**

Preparation time **30 minutes**, plus cooling

Cooking time **about 2½ hours**

1 tablespoon **sunflower oil**

750 g (1½ lb) diced **stewing beef**, any fat discarded

4 **smoked streaky bacon rashers**, diced

1 **onion**, chopped

200 ml (7 fl oz) **red wine**

400 ml (14 fl oz) **beef stock**

1 tablespoon **tomato purée**

2 teaspoons **mustard powder**

6 **bay leaves**

1 tablespoon **cornflour**, mixed with a little water

25 g (1 oz) **butter**

250 g (8 oz) **shallots**, halved if large

1 quantity **gluten-free pastry** (see page 13) with 1 teaspoon dry mustard powder added

beaten egg, to glaze

salt and **pepper**

Heat the oil in a frying pan and add the beef, a few pieces at a time, until it has all been added to the pan. Fry over a high heat, stirring until browned on all sides. Lift out of the pan and transfer to a casserole dish.

Fry the bacon and onion until golden, then add the wine, stock, tomato purée and mustard powder. Add 2 bay leaves and season generously with salt and pepper. Add the cornflour mix, bring to the boil, stirring until thickened, then pour over the beef.

Cover the casserole dish and bake in a preheated oven, 180°C (350°F), Gas Mark 4, for 2 hours until the beef is very tender. Heat the butter in a clean frying pan and fry the shallots until golden (about 5 minutes). Add to the beef casserole and leave to cool.

Divide the beef mixture between 4 × 300 ml (½ pint) individual ovenproof pie dishes. Cut the pastry into 4, roll one piece out between 2 sheets of clingfilm for a pie lid. Brush the rim of a dish with beaten egg, remove one sheet of clingfilm, lay the pastry over the dish, then remove the top sheet of clingfilm. Press the pastry on to the dish edge with fingers dusted with rice flour. Trim off the excess pastry and fork the edge. Repeat until 4 pies have been made. Brush with egg, add a bay leaf to each for decoration, then bake in a preheated oven, 190°C (375°F), Gas Mark 5, for 20–25 minutes until the pastry is golden and the filling piping hot.

For beery beef & mustard pies, omit the red wine and add 300 ml (½ pint) bitter or other strong beer and 300 ml (½ pint) beef stock. Omit the shallots and add 3 sliced portabella mushrooms. Continue as above.

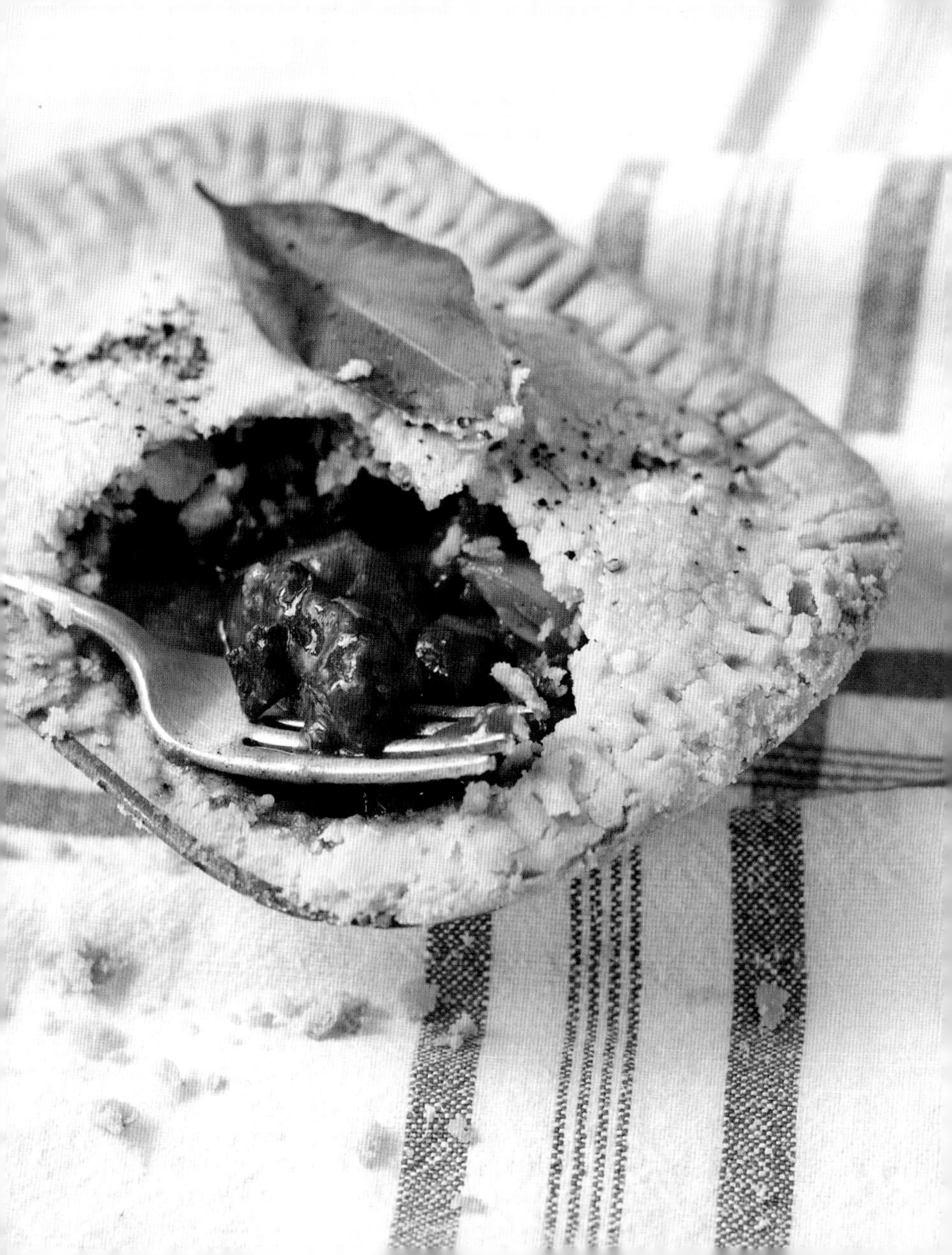

glazed apple tart

Serves **8**

Preparation time **30 minutes**, plus chilling

Cooking time **1 hour–1 hour 10 minutes**

1 quantity **sweet gluten-free pastry** (see page 13)

3 **cooking apples**, about 625 g (1¼ lb)

125 g (4 oz) **caster sugar**

3 **eggs**

grated rind and juice of 1 **lemon**

2 tablespoons **fine-cut marmalade**

Press the just-made pastry over the base and sides of a buttered 24 cm (9½ inch) fluted loose-bottomed tart tin, using fingers dusted in rice flour, until the pastry is an even thickness and stands a little above the top of the tin. Trim with scissors to neaten if needed. Prick the base with a fork, put on a baking sheet and chill for 15 minutes.

Line the tart case with nonstick baking paper, add baking beans and bake blind in a preheated oven, 190°C (375°F), Gas Mark 5, for 10 minutes. Remove the paper and beans and cook for a further 5 minutes. Reduce the oven temperature to 180°C (350°F) Gas Mark 4.

Quarter, core and peel the apples, cut into thin slices and arrange slightly overlapping in rings over the base of the tart, then top with a second layer. Reserve 25 g (1 oz) of the sugar for the topping, then mix the rest with the eggs, lemon rind and juice, beating with a fork until smooth. Pour over the apples.

Sprinkle with the remaining sugar, then bake for 40–45 minutes until the apples are browned and the pastry base is cooked through. Brush the marmalade over the top and return the tart to the oven and bake for a further 5–10 minutes until glistening.

For glazed apricot tart, fill the baked blind tart case with 500 g (1 lb) halved and stoned apricots. Mix 3 eggs with 75 g (3 oz) sugar and the grated rind and juice of 1 lemon, then pour over the apricots. Sprinkle with 15 g (½ oz) extra sugar and bake as above. Glaze with 2 tablespoons warmed apricot jam after cooking.

lemon meringue pies

Makes **6**

Preparation time **30 minutes**, plus chilling

Cooking time **25–30 minutes**

1 quantity **sweet gluten-free pastry** (see page 13)

400 g (13 oz) can **full-fat condensed milk**

3 **egg yolks**

grated rind of 2 **lemons**

4 tablespoons **lemon juice**

4 **egg whites**

125 g (4 oz) **caster sugar**

Cut the pastry into 6, then roll one portion out between 2 sheets of clingfilm until a little larger than a buttered individual 10 cm (4 inch) loose-bottomed fluted tart tin. Remove one sheet of clingfilm, lay the pastry over the tin, then remove the top sheet of clingfilm. Press the pastry into the base and sides of the tin with fingers dusted with rice flour. Trim off the excess pastry with scissors so that it stands a little above the top of the tin. Patch any cracks or breaks with pastry trimmings. Repeat to make 6 tarts. Prick the bases with a fork, then chill for 15 minutes.

Bake the tarts blind (see page 15) for 10 minutes. Remove the paper and baking beans and cook for a further 5 minutes. Remove from the oven, and reduce the oven temperature to 180°C (350°F), Gas Mark 4.

Mix the condensed milk, egg yolks, lemon rind and juice together in a bowl until the mixture thickens, then spoon the filling into the tart cases. In a second bowl, whisk the egg whites until stiff, then gradually whisk in the sugar, a little at a time until very thick and glossy.

Spoon the meringue over the lemon filling and swirl with the back of a spoon into peaks. Bake for 10–15 minutes until the meringue peaks are golden and just set. Leave to stand for 5 minutes, then remove from the tins and serve warm or cold with cream.

For St Clements meringue pies, mix the condensed milk with the egg yolks, the grated rinds of 1 orange, 1 lemon and 1 lime, and 4 tablespoons of mixed fruit juice. Spoon into the 6 baked tart cases. Make the meringue with 4 egg whites and 125 g (4 oz) mixed caster sugar and light muscovado sugar. Bake as above.

banoffee pie

Serves **6**

Preparation time **25 minutes**, plus chilling

Cooking time **4–5 minutes**

150 g (5 oz) packet **rich tea gluten-free biscuits**

65 g (2½ oz) **butter**

1 tablespoon **golden syrup**

300 ml (½ pint) **double cream**

2 **bananas**

juice of ½ **lemon**

For the toffee filling

100 g (3½ oz) **butter**

100 g (3½ oz) **dark muscovado sugar**

400 g (13 oz) can **full-fat condensed milk**

To decorate

diced **toffees**

grated **chocolate** (optional)

Crush the biscuits in a plastic bag using a rolling pin. Melt the butter in a saucepan with the syrup, take off the heat and stir in the biscuit crumbs. Tip into an unbuttered 20 cm (8 inch) fluted loose-bottomed tart tin, then press over the base and up the sides with the back of a spoon to make into an even layer. Chill for 30 minutes.

Make the toffee filling. Melt the butter in a clean dry pan with the sugar, add the condensed milk and stir well, then bring to the boil and cook over a medium heat for 4–5 minutes, stirring constantly, until the mixture begins to thicken, smells of toffee and crystallizes around the edges. Be careful not to overheat or the milk can scorch easily.

Pour the toffee into the pie case, leave to cool, then chill for 3½–4½ hours or until ready to serve.

Whip the cream until it forms soft swirls. Slice the bananas and toss with the lemon juice, then fold into the cream and spoon over the pie. Decorate the top with diced toffees and grated chocolate, if liked. Serve within 2 hours of decorating.

For toffee chocolate pie, make up the pie case and toffee layer as above. Melt 100 g (3½ oz) plain dark chocolate in a bowl over hot water, then stir in the (unwhipped) cream and 2 tablespoons icing sugar. Chill for 30 minutes, then whisk until just beginning to thicken, spoon over the toffee layer and sprinkle with roughly chopped toasted hazelnuts.

pear & frangipane tart

Serves **6-8**

Preparation time **30 minutes**, plus chilling

Cooking time **45–55 minutes**

1 quantity **sweet gluten-free pastry** (see page 13)

125 g (4 oz) **butter**, at room temperature

125 g (4 oz) **caster sugar**

125 g (4 oz) **ground almonds**

2 **eggs**

few drops of **almond essence**

100 g (3½ oz) **plain dark chocolate**, diced

4 ripe **pears**, quartered, cored, peeled and thickly sliced

juice of ½ **lemon**

2 tablespoons **flaked almonds**

sifted **icing sugar**, for dusting

Press the just-made pastry over the base and up the sides of a buttered 24 cm (9½ inch) fluted loose-bottomed tart tin using fingers dusted in rice flour until the pastry stands a little above the top of the tin. Trim with scissors to neaten. Prick the base with a fork, put on a baking sheet and chill for 15 minutes.

Bake the tart blind (see page 15) for 10 minutes. Remove the paper and baking beans and cook for a further 5 minutes. Remove from the oven, and reduce the oven temperature to 180°C (350°F), Gas Mark 4.

Cream the butter and sugar together until light and fluffy. Add the ground almonds, eggs and almond essence and beat until smooth. Fold in half the chocolate.

Toss the pears in the lemon juice and arrange half in a random pattern in the base of the tart. Spoon the almond frangipane over the top and spread as evenly as you can. Press the remaining pears into the filling, then sprinkle with the flaked almonds. Bake for 30–40 minutes until the frangipane is golden and just set. Check after 20 minutes and cover the top loosely with foil if the almonds seem to be browning too quickly. Leave to cool for 30 minutes.

Remove the tart from the tin, sprinkle with the remaining chocolate and dust with icing sugar. Serve warm or cold.

For chocolate sauce, to serve as an accompaniment, break 100 g (3½ oz) dark chocolate into pieces and melt in a bowl set over a saucepan of gently simmering water with 50 g (2 oz) unsalted butter and 1 tablespoon golden syrup. Cool slightly, then spoon over the tart.

mincemeat, apricot & apple pies

Makes **12**
Preparation time **30 minutes**
Cooking time **20 minutes**

1 quantity **sweet gluten-free
  pastry** (see page 13)
  flavoured with 1 teaspoon
  ground cinnamon
125 g (4 oz) **gluten-free fruit
  mincemeat**
75 g (3 oz) **ready-to-eat
  dried apricots**, diced
1 **dessert apple**, peeled,
  cored and finely chopped
egg white, to glaze
sifted **icing sugar**, for dusting

Reserve one-third of the pastry. Cut the rest in half,
and roll one half out between 2 sheets of clingfilm
until 5 mm (¼ inch) thick. Stamp out as many 6 cm
(2½ inch) circles with a fluted biscuit cutter as you
can, peel off the clingfilm and press into the buttered
sections of a 12-section bun tin with your fingers
dusted with rice flour. Roll out the other pastry half and
repeat until you have 12 pie cases. Add the trimmings
to the reserved pastry.

Mix the mincemeat with the apricots and apple, then
spoon into the pie cases. Roll out the remaining pastry
between clingfilm as before, then cut out 12 × 5 cm
(2 inch) star shapes, add to the pie tops and brush
with egg white.

Bake in a preheated oven, 190°C (375°F), Gas Mark 5,
for about 20 minutes until golden. Leave to stand for
10 minutes, then loosen the edges with a small knife
and lift out of the tin (the pies are more crumbly than
those made with wheat flour, so take extra care). Leave
to cool completely on a wire rack, then dust with icing
sugar before serving.

For almond mince pies, add 25 g (1 oz) ground
almonds to the pastry instead of the ground cinnamon.
Top the filling with 40 g (1½ oz) flaked almonds, then
bake as above, covering with foil after 15 minutes if
the almonds seem to be browning too quickly. Dust
with icing sugar to serve.

index

acknowledgements

Executive editor Eleanor Maxfield
Senior editor Sybella Stephens
Art direction & design Tracy Killick
Photographer Stephen Conroy
Home economist Sara Lewis
Prop stylist Rachel Jukes
Production Caroline Alberti

Photography copyright © Octopus Publishing Group
Limited/Stephen Conroy, except the following:
copyright © Octopus Publishing Group/David Munns
105; Ian Wallace 167, 189, 195, 199, 201;
Lis Parsons 57, 83, 169; Will Heap 15-17, 53, 133,
137, 141, 149, 153, 179, 193, 203, 214;
William Shaw 39, 47, 58, 91, 107, 120, 160, 187.